OBSESSIVE MEMORIES

Also by Clara Maslow

Schlepper

When the Lilacs Last Bloomed I Mourned

The Tapestry of our Lives Torn with Fear

OBSESSIVE
MEMORIES

Remembering My Father Yalek Who Never Told Me about Love

CLARA R. MASLOW

iUniverse LLC
Bloomington

Obsessive Memories
Remembering My Father Yalek Who Never Told Me about Love

iUniverse books may be ordered through booksellers or by contacting:

iUniverse LLC
1663 Liberty Drive
Bloomington, IN 47403
www.iuniverse.com
1-800-Authors (1-800-288-4677)

Because of the dynamic nature of the Internet, any web addresses or links contained in this book may have changed since publication and may no longer be valid. The views expressed in this work are solely those of the author and do not necessarily reflect the views of the publisher, and the publisher hereby disclaims any responsibility for them.

Any people depicted in stock imagery provided by Thinkstock are models, and such images are being used for illustrative purposes only.
Certain stock imagery © Thinkstock.

ISBN: 978-1-4917-0642-8 (sc)
ISBN: 978-1-4917-0704-3 (hc)
ISBN: 978-1-4917-0703-6 (e)

Library of Congress Control Number: 2013916551

Printed in the United States of America

iUniverse rev. date: 09/27/2013

CONTENTS

The moral we should draw from the European past, and in particular from Christianity, is not instruction about the authority under which should live but suggestions about how to make ourselves wonderfully different from anything that has been.

—Richard Rorty

DEDICATION

FOR MY FATHER YALEK

This is a book of remembering my father Yalek, who was a highly intelligent, intellectual man with exceptional talents in the creative arts, in architectural drawing and construction. But he did not talk, he never told me about love. I never saw love expressed. It tool me a lifetime to know that I loved him, and to understand him in order to understand myself, to know that I identified with him, with his talents. To understand that my own talents in the creative arts were his legacy to me.

FOR MY MOTHER RIVA

For Riva, a beautiful woman, mother, and a wonderful role model. She loved everyone and she taught us to love everyone. She was the exceptionally generous and giving and most devoted being.
She taught us all to care, to be devoted. She was an extraordinary role model for us.

FOR Emily Cohen, my Granddaughter and for Talya, my Great Granddaughter

Emily, my granddaughter, who has followed in the tradition of the female role models in our family legacy, after Riva and Ida, and of myself. The female model she now embodies, of a loving, caring woman. I am grateful that she has become a woman in our family tradition, a deeply devoted woman. And mother of Talya.

FEELINGS OF SAUDADE

The elephant Suleiman is on a journey a long trip
everything is calm
He is no ordinary elephant, he is ancient, born
in the regal court, called Solomon
His mahout is named Subhro together they are whispering
in a tongue known only to them

Solomon is slowly plodding up the ancient mountain
overlooking the deep blue sea
A gentle story as a skiff pulling up to a river bank
slowly, passing ox-carts on sunburned plains
in swirling mists with wolves and snows
Subhro is not an Indian, but a faithful peasant in thrall
with saudade, the essentially Portuguese
feeling of yearning

Overcome with saudade, feelings of yearning
yearning to be with you holding hands
on that winding road from Mytilene turning round
the mountain covered with twisted olive trees
winding down to Petra and the deep blue sea

At every twisting turn a marker miniature shrine
to remember those that died there
I yearn to be with you in Petra to stand in the tiny chapel
on the mountain top looking across the clear blue sea
making love in the afternoon beneath the fan, shades drawn
Into eternity

Wandering the garden at end of day
with feelings of saudade yearning for you

By Clara Maslow
November 10, 2011

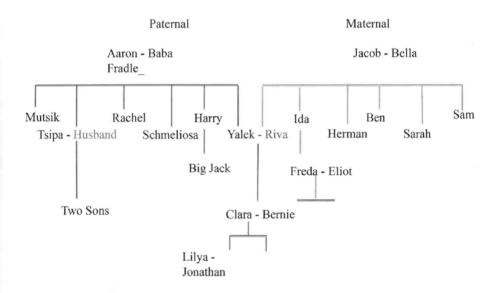

Paternal

Aaron - Baba
Fradle_

Maternal

Jacob - Bella

Mutsik

Tsipa - Husband

Rachel

Schmeliosa

Big Jack

Harry

Yalek - Riva

Ida

Herman

Freda - Eliot

Ben

Sarah

Sam

Two Sons

Clara - Bernie

Lilya -
Jonathan

PREFACE

In the early years growing up I spent much time watching my father Yalek. He was so neat and clean when he worked doing the repairs and maintenance around the house And he was social in his talking to neighbors and his tenants . He was a handsome man tall and well built with dark hair and beautiful green eyes, which I inherited. And he moved so lithely, even when he was repairing the roof of the house.

I also knew the stories that my mother Riva told us, with The Baba in the kitchen, evenings, in Yiddish, their first language. She cried bitterly when she told of how Yalek was beaten by his mother Babe Fradle and sent to sleep in the chicken coops. He was the oldest of six children, to Babe Fradle and his father Aaron and the most intelligent and talented. He was talented in the creative visual arts, in architectural drawings, in construction, and china decorating.

I also knew , watching him so closely that he did not talk to us, he was not articulate. That I never heard words of love, or saw any exhibition of love between them. Even though I knew from my mother how passionately they loved each other. I knew that every morning I saw him roll up his pillow in the blanket and carry it from the sofa to the bedroom.

I knew that I resembled my father Yalek in many ways; I was intelligent, and I was talented in the same ways. I Identified with him but I was bothered by his being inarticulate, and unable to talk to me of love.

I studied foreign cultures and particularly the child rearing practices of foreign culture, such as the Irish, the Polish, the countries of the Middle East, and others. I learned that the severe practice of beating children to teach them to behave was detrimental to their development as adults with the inability to have good loving relationships.

I thought that if I could understand my life I could embrace it with some degree of joy. An element that I needed greatly in a family of closely knit young devoted immigrants, whose lives were filled with turmoil and tragedy in making their place in this country.

CHAPTER I

INDIVIDUALITY

Who am I? Am I as beautiful as my mother Riva? Do I look more like my handsome father Yalek's family? Like most young people growing up I have wanted an identity. I wanted to know who I looked like, who I resembled?

Who I inherited my intellect from? What kind of person would I be? It had also to do with the need to be independent.

I don't know about other children but I was concerned.

I was trying to put the pieces together to have some harmony, the psychic, social, and cosmic harmony.

I was the first born child into a close knit family of young immigrants. From Riva's side, the grandparents Jacob and Bella. And from Yalek's side, Babe Fradle and Aaron. There was no particular association with the Jewish Orthodox religion on either side. There was no legacy there.

There was a Jewish humanism which was a faith in the goodness of human beings.

They did not look to spiritual security. They preferred the goodness of humans.

I remember as a young girl growing up thinking about what I was thinking about. It has been a difficult concept to explain, to family, to friends. But as I grew older and learned more about the people in my family I was more comfortable with the idea. I was no longer afraid to feel different.

"The proper time frame" has been a marker for historians for centuries. "The same mistakes that we made are still being made" is still being repeated. And yet they are still being carried on. What was happening in the world around was of interest to the family and thus to me. In our family of news readers the young and the old, everyone was interested. We needed to know because that was the culture of our family life.

Discussion, discussion, discussion.

"Each of us is the child of our times. Human nature is not a timeless essence, but is penetrated through and through by our historical situation." (Siegfried Hegel, 1886)

As a child I remember growing up in a tightly knit, interdependent, closely devoted family of immigrants recently arrived in this country. We were living in an attached house, in row housing in the working class neighborhood of Trenton, (NJ). It was my father Yalek, and his brother Harry, and my mother Riva, and her mother The Baba, and all her five siblings.

I was the first child born to the beautiful Riva and the handsome Yalek. It was the union of two prominent families of Baranovka (Russia), Each one was the oldest of their familiy of six children. They were born in Baranovka, and grew up there. They fell in love when they were young; they married there and shortly after Yalek immigrated to the United States with his brother Harry. Riva stayed behind they did not have enough money for passage for both. The plan was for Yalek to get work, and to save money from his salary for him to send to Riva for passage for her and for her family.

Riva's younger sister Ida arrived here a young girl of eighteen. She was not married. She landed a job in the Garment Industry in NYC as assistant dress designer. She was exceptionally talented as dress designer and dress maker since early childhood. She had spent her early years designing and making clothes for everyone in the family. She inherited her great talents from her father Jacob who was a shoe designer and maker in Baranovka.

Ida and Harry were not joined until later, the two sisters with the two brothers. Big Jack was their first child, that is why we called him "Big". And he was the first male child of Riva's siblings named after Jacob. My brother was the second male child. And he was called "Little" Jack. Then came the third male child born to Riva's brother Herman (and wife). He was called "Sonny". Then was the fourth child named after Jacob, It was Ben's (and Clara's) son, Jack.

I was the oldest of the grandchildren born into this intermarried family. It was a closely knit, closely devoted family. Everyone, my mother Riva, and sister Ida, and The Baba were in close touch on a daily basis. Each one caring for the others, and their children. I grew up amidst the tumult of chattering children, of hovering adults, of my mother and The Baba telling stories, mostly in Yiddish, about life in Baranovka every evening at the kitchen table.

And I remember Yalek as an intelligent and educated man, and a reader. After his day's work, he read three Yiddish newspapers daily. He was learning to read the daily English newspaper as well. And I remember when their friends from Baranovka came to visit us, from Philadelphia where they had settled, the conversation was lively, and mostly about world politics, and what it means. They were immigrants, they were intelligent and enlightened.

I remember when I was about twenty, a boy friend took me with him to a meeting at Columbia University in August. It was the first meeting of a group of students gathering from many schools who wanted to establish the organization known as The National Student League. The goal was to have a national group to keep the students informed about current issues in politics across the country. The information was to be written by the most prominent, the best journalists in the leading journals.

It was an interesting and stimulating meeting and an opportunity to hear from the students themselves across the country, on such important matters. For me it was an exciting opportunity to listen to the best thinking students. I learned many things. I learned where to get information on a daily basis and what to read. I learned how to become the person I wanted to be. I learned to respect my parents' intellectual background and their legacy.

When I first met Bern—Isaac, his father, had arranged for him to come to Belmar (NJ), to our summer home to meet me. He was wearing a sailor's uniform, and a big old-fashioned hearing aid, a big metal box that hung from his waist on his leather belt. He explained that he had many ear infections when he was a little boy. At that time the doctors did not know how to relieve ear infections. There were no antibiotic medications. Each time the doctor had to puncture the ear drum to let out the infection. After each puncture, the ear drum thickened and could not vibrate. Consequently Bern had a 50 percent hearing loss in both ears. He went through high school with this hearing loss, graduating at age fifteen, then on to CCNY where he graduated with MS in Mechanical Engineering at 20. And then to his first job at 20.

After Bern and I were married, we talked about the War (World War II). Many young men we knew were being drafted. Both my brother Little Jack, and Big Jack had been drafted. And, knowing Bern's hearing loss condition we judged he would not be taken.

Bern's draft number came up, He reported to the Draft Board. He was examined, and told the Officer of his considerable hearing loss. Nevertheless he was drafted into the US Navy. During the interview the Officer discovered that Bern was a highly experienced engineer.

At that time, early in the War, the Navy was greatly in need of engineers. When he returned from the draft board examination. When he returned home he told us he had been drafted into the Navy. He served his term at the Naval Station in Norfolk, Va.

THE SAILOR SUIT

On a weekend leave and dressed in his Sailor Suit, Bern took me to The Café Society Nightclub. This was a new nightclub; there was one in the Village (Downtown), and one Uptown, in area of 42nd St. Bern's friends were a group of young intellectual New Yorkers who loved music. They loved Jazz especially, and at that time, they loved all the black musicians who played jazz. They knew about the opening of Café Society and that the owner of the club, who happened to be from Trenton, was the first nightclub owner in the city to allow black musicians to play in his night club.

The roster of musicians playing at Cafe Society was astonishing. Among the famous artists who played were Paul Robeson, Billie Holiday, Mary Lou Williams, and Lena Horne.

Many years later, when our granddaughter Emily was grown, she came to live with me. Bern wanted her to know how much he loved me. He wrote her a letter telling her about the time he took me to Café Society, wearing a Sailor Suit, with his friends to hear the greatest Jazz music of the day.

He said, "As we were being shown to a table, it was as though there was a sudden hush as heads swiveled around to admire the luminous blonde beauty escorted by the guy in the sailor suit, And I felt a surge of pride that I was privileged to have a share of this work. And as the years went on, I was able to feel even greater pride in her accomplishments, And despite the rocky periods we went through we could turn to each other and say, "I love you so much, I am glad I married you."

And I remember going to Café Society again with Bern and his friends to hear Paul Robeson, one of the greatest singers of America. I had never heard anything like his voice before. His voice was, exquisite and splendid—the most wonderfully magnificent voice I had ever heard. I knew I was privileged to hear him in person.

Subsequently I heard him sing at the Metropolitan Opera where he now appeared regularly. And this too was an unforgettable experience. For me, growing up in a rural environment, it meant a great deal to be able to hear Paul Robeson sing at the Metropolitan. He was one of the greatest singers America produced.

In retrospect, I feel like I was growing up in a high cultural environment. I grew up in a rather small family of highly intellectual and highly cultured people. People who appreciated and listened to classical symphony music constantly. My Aunt Ida, my mother Riva's sister was an opera goer in New York. She attended concerts and opera with her friends whom she met in the Garment factories, on a regular basis.

It was Ida who arranged (and paid for) her child Freda and me (her niece) to go to NYC every week for piano lessons and to go to the Children's Philharmonic Symphony concerts every week. Every Saturday morning I would take Freda by the hand, we boarded the train to NYC, go uptown to Carnegie Hall, where we would each have a piano lesson. Then we would go for lunch, and then in the afternoon we would attend the concerts of the Children's Philharmonic Orchestra.

As a family we were steeped in classical music. Freda majored in music when she attended college. She graduated a music major. All through her married life she had annual tickets to the Metropolitan Opera. She attended regularly.

Bern was also a musical child, from a musical family. His parents provided him with piano lessons at age five. I see the past differently as I grow older. So in a sense the past changes. The high emotional tone of the experience at The Café Society—its dramatic importance, listening to Jazz music by the greatest performers of the day,—is a most memorable experience.

While we were courting, Bern took me to the concerts at the Lewisohn Stadium. This was an outdoor concert stadium on bleachers in the Bronx. It was New York City, free concerts for the public every summer. The concerts were combined some with the Philharmonic Orchestra, featuring classical music. At other times the concerts featured the Music of Broadway and its singers. Listening to music at the Lewisohn Stadium, on the outdoor bleachers was a breathtaking experience. Listening to the grand symphonies, sitting on the bleachers in the cool evenings of summer, listening under the stars, holding hands with Bern. I felt privileged. I loved it.

After we moved north to Concord, Mass. Bern found the Handel-Hayden Society choral group concerts. We attended regularly for many years. We loved the concerts of classical music. We especially loved the Handel's 'MESSIAH" every year.

In her memoir Pentimento, published in 1973, Lillian Hellman wrote,

> Old paint on canvas, as it ages, sometimes becomes transparent. When that happens, it is possible to see the original lines; a tree will show through a woman's dress, a large boat is no longer on the open sea. That is called pentimento. The painter" "repented", changed his mind. It is a way of seeing, then seeing again.

For me this way of thinking, of 'thinking again' is most interesting. I recall that in my early years I remember 'a way of thinking about what I was thinking about.' And I knew very few people who would understand this concept. I found it useful and satisfying and helpful.

And now, much later, I have found someone who is expressing this 'thinking again', Or 'seeing again'.

In thinking of my obsessive memories of my father Yalek, I have thought of him and his daily ritual. Every morning I would see him rolling up the pillow in the blanket and moving them both to the bedroom. There have also been the obsessive memories of his silence and of being inarticulate with his children—of my never hearing words of love or affection expressed. I have needed another way of "seeing" these acts expressed, a way that is more generous and more loving in their interpretations.

For many years Bern and I went to Greece for summer vacations. Ever since I was a teen-ager, I had been reading the stories about the beauty of the Greek Islands, about the archeological places and about the special beauty of the Aegean Sea. But I would not consider visiting Greece while the undemocratic rulers, the members of the Junta, were in power. It was an ideological issue with me.

Finally after a seven-year dictatorship, the Junta was voted out. A parliamentary democracy was put in its place with Alexander Papandraou as the new President. I felt as if the curtain was lifted, and things were now possible. And the opportunity soon came along.

A small academic publication of political economics which I subscribed to, was also watching this change in government. As soon as Papandraou was elected President they offered a Tour in Greece.

It was a two week tour, including a week of seeing the important archaeological places.

I signed up for us right away.

We spent five days in Athens, each day visiting different historical places. Then the group was flown to the Island of Mytilene, to a village called Petra in the northern Aegean. Petra is a very old small fishing village in the Aegean. We could see the coast of Turkey as we sat on the patio every evening having dinner. The views of the sunset over the Aegean is so beautiful it is thrilling.

It is one of the most beautiful I have seen. Bern and I were very happy here.

In Petra, were greeted by a group of thirty five women. There was no hotel or motel in Petra, not even a Bed and Breakfast place. And no one, except one woman spoke English. Her name was Helen. Her Husband was George. He and his family had lived in Petra for generations. His family still lived there, and he owned land there. He and Helen were building a motel, the first in Petra.

The thirty five women represented a Women's Group formed to bring Tourism to Petra. Under the new democratic government of Papandraou, they had received a large grant to help the people in the village to build rooms with bathrooms, new accommodations for tourism. We were the first group of tourists under this new grant. Because the places were not built we stayed in the homes of the Women's Group. Each couple in a woman's home.

We had breakfast in the host woman's home—a large Greek-style breakfast, including homemade yogurt with homemade honey. Then we were taken in several very old fishing boats—possibly a hundred years old—to the uninhabited islands for a picnic lunch. The women pulled Sea Conch out of the water, removed the fish which was served with homemade feta cheeses, and homemade bread from the town bakery, with fruit and lots of homemade wine.

For the evening dinner, which was served in a Taverna, a large Tavern, it was family style. All the women cooked the classic Greek dishes, prepared a sumptuous dinner. All this was accompanied with music and singing, and after dinner there was dancing. and lots of homemade wine.

The most fun we had was in how we managed to talk to each other using our different languages. The people were gracious and generous and they wanted to provide us with wonderful pleasurable memories. And indeed these were exceptional and wonderful memories.

This was truly a place for vacationing lovers, and for people interested in ancient history of the Greek Isles. It was the old Isle of Sappho, the Greek poet of love.

There are many good memories in my long life. Going every summer to Petra to visit our Greek friends, to swim in the beautiful Aegean Sea, and to make love under the fan, on the Isle of Lesbos—where long ago Sappho made love—was most memorable.

Left: My father, Yalek
Right: Me sitting on my mother, Riva

CHAPTER II

MY FATHER YALEK, A LONG JOURNEY TO BELMAR

Into my heart an air that kills from yon far country blows,
What are those blue remembered hills, what spires what
farms are those?
That is the land of last content, I see it shining plain, the
happy highways
Where I went and cannot come again. A. E. Housman

Into my heart on air with a poets thinking comes the story of my
father Yalek. A handsome young man about 20, out of Baranovka,
Russia. He has just been married to Riva his love, and he is about to
leave his home to take his long independent journey to the US. He
is leaving to establish a home for Riva his new wife and a family to
come. The year is 1905

Remembering the stories told by my mother Riva, and my grandma The Baba as they told us in the kitchen every evening, in Yiddish their own language. The stories are about Yalek and Riva growing up in two families in Baranovka, Russia, falling in love when they were young, marrying and soon Yalek leaving for the US to establish a new life.

I can see the hills and the farms of the town, a happy town of mostly Jewish families. Baranovka was a small town, little bigger than a shtetle, located in the Crimea region of Russia, near Kiev. The region was well known for its exceptionally fertile agricultural land which produced large harvests of wheat, and corn that was exported across the world. The families of the town, the residents owned their own homes, they were self supporting. Many had large farms with orchards and livestock. They were economically independent.

Yalek was a handsome young man, tall and strong, with dark hair and beautiful green eyes. He was known to be intelligent, well educated and known from early on to be a talented child. His special talents were hand decorating, architectural drawing, painting, and he was skilled in building and constructing. He was the oldest of six children of Babe Fradle and Aaron, his father. When he was 14 his parents recognized his talents and sent him to Kiev, the large industrial city nearby to a Fabricant to learn to decorate fine china. He became skilled in this art. He learned the skills of architectural drawing on his own, and the skills of construction on his own as well. He learned business skills from his father Aaron, who sold Real Estate.

The family of Babe Fradle and Aaron lived on a large farm, of several acres, which had a few orchards, with many fruit trees, with large vegetable and flower gardens and cows and chickens. Babe Fradle managed the farm herself with help from her children. She was a large handsome woman with distinctive deep set blue eyes.

She was known in the town as an authoritarian personality, who ruled her family with a stick, and a strong temper.

Aaron was a mild tempered easy going, and generous person. His children loved him. After Babe Fradle died in Russia, Aaron emigrated to the US, He lived in Newark, near Yalek. He remarried and was a happy man. He visited us frequently.

Babe Fradle favored Harry her second son who looked like her. He was a heavy man, overweight, with the same distinctive deep blue eyes as his mother. When she was angered she punished Yalek by beating him severely with a stick. And she sent him to sleep in the chicken coops. Riva said that Yalek suffered from these beatings. She cried for him.

When Riva tells the story of Yalek and how Babe Fradle beat him physically, and sent him to sleep in the chicken coops—She cries bitterly. She knew Yalek, they grew up together, She loved him deeply, passionately. She knew that he was badly hurt. She felt his hurting.

Riva was the oldest of six children of Jacob, and Babe Bella.

Jacob was a most handsome man, tall with blonde hair, blue eyes. He was a talented man—a shoe designer and maker. And he was intelligent, educated, an intellectual who spent most of his time in the synagogue discussing philosophy, history and politics with the other intellectuals of the community. At the time they were the knew "humanists". They were known as the new Jewish "Atheists." The children of Jacob and Babe Bella were all intellectual and educated. They were known in the town as intellectuals.

Riva was a beautiful woman who resembled her father. She was tall, with a lovely figure with bright red hair and blue eyes. She was an exceptional woman, an exceptional human being. She was bright, extremely devoted, giving and generous. And she was extremely devoted and loving with her siblings and their families. She and Yalek fell in love when they were young. They married and soon he left for the US

It was the early twentieth century, a long time of political unrest and upheaval in many Eastern European countries and particularly in Russia under the rule of the Czar, a vicious monarchy. It was a time when new movements initiated by the indigent people such as communism, totalitarianism and fascism were beginning to take hold. But it was also a time when the young people were interested in democracy, in the democratic form of government for themselves, and for their future families. The young people of Yalek's generation, who grew up under a czarist regime were most anxious to leave. They suffered years of bitter repression In many cases they needed to leave as many were being hunted by the police. Not for crimes but for minor infractions. They needed to get out of the country. Yalek was one of a large number who ran away.

As Gabriel Garcia Marquez said, "We recall our lives through our long built up memories. Life is not what one has lived through but what one remembers and how one remembers it in order to tell it."

In my mind's eye, the poet's eye, I see clearly the young handsome Yalek with his brother Harry as they landed in New York City in 1905. They soon found their way to Trenton, New Jersey, where Yalek got a job as china decorator with the Great Lenox China Ltd. Company, now known as Lenox Corporation. Harry also got a job there but not as a decorator.

As soon as he started to work Yalek started to save his money for passage for Riva and her family to come to the United States. He had learned as a child how to be frugal from his mother Babe Fradle, watching her manage her large family, and manage the large farm as well. And he had learned watching his father Aaron how to manage money, since Aaron sold real estate to make a living.

In fact, most families in Baranovka were workers, farmers or business men. That is how they made a living. They all lived frugally. There was no aristocracy in a Jewish town. It was an organized community, a group of people who lived harmoniously. They owned their own homes, they grew their own food, they provided education for their children with the synagogue as the center. Baranovka was culturally a model Jewish town. It was eliminated in World War II. It was "bombed out".

I remember the stories Riva told us of how Yalek saved his wages, down to the last penny. He never spent any money on himself. He always said that he did not need anything.

Finally, he had sent enough for Riva and The Baba and all the five siblings to come to the US. Jacob, their father did not come, he had died in a Flu epidemic the year before they left. The family settled In Trenton. Yalek had rented a house, a row house in a working class neighborhood, that was big enough to accommodate all of them.

Then Yalek continued to save his money for passage to the US for his father Aaron, and for his siblings, Rachel and Shmielyosa. They all came to live in New Jersey, to be near Yalek.

Then he began to save for a house for his own family. And finally he began to save for a used car. Of course he had a plan. Yalek was a planner personality by nature, he always planned ahead, He figured out what he wanted to do and how to do it. Knowing how to do architectural drawings was his special talent and was particularly helpful—his basic ability for planning.

While growing up, Yalek had watched his father Aaron closely. Aaron had his own real estate business. Yalek observed and learned about the financial aspects. How transactions could provide profit for the owner. In other words, if you own a house and rent it, this can provide a profit for the owner. This was very intriguing for Yalek. He wanted to provide for his family, in the best possible way and from the rent income. It was important to him, his responsibility, to be able to provide for his children's education.

Yalek also remembered when he was growing up, as a young boy he loved swimming in the Black Sea. He thought a great deal about having a summer house, near the ocean for his children to swim in the ocean. To be strong swimmers and healthy. But he knew that he could not do this on his working man's wages. He needed an income property, a property that he could rent-out and have an income. There was planning, a great deal of planning to be done.

First, he needed a car to find the ocean. Then, he needed to buy a property, to build the house/apartments for his family, and to rent for income. He needed a property to bring in the income to pay for all this. The times were favorable. It was the early 20th c. It coincided with the development of the real estate along the New Jersey shore—north from the northern coast down the coast to the end of New Jersey. The federal and state governments were at this time planning on building the large state highways, from north to south; from Maine to Florida, to make the shore and ocean accessible for the public to enjoy.

Yalek was a visionary, a planner into the future. His plans for providing a summer home for his family, his wife Riva and children at the seashore so that they could swim and be healthy was coincidental with the planning of the federal and state governments up and down the Eastern Coast of the US. It happened at the same time.

Yalek did buy a used car. And soon he found the ocean at Belmar, New Jersey, a small coastal town that was due east from Trenton, where they lived. It was a town on the ocean front just south of Asbury Park a main city. This was just the time when the Federal and State Governments up and down the eastern coast, from Maine to Florida, were planning the major highways. They needed to open up the land with major highways that would make access to the ocean possible for the entire population.

It was a good time to be looking for land, property was cheap. And Yalek was lucky. the first year, when I was just a toddler of eighteen months, Yalek and Riva rented a bungalow in Belmar. It was the beginning.

The bungalow was a long way from the ocean, the path—the land between the houses and the ocean was wide—Up and down the coast, (guessing) about a block and a half. It was covered with wild shrubs—wild huckleberry, wild blueberry, wild flowering shrubs. There was a path for walking open to the beach and ocean.

Every day Riva would push me in the carriage from the house along the path to the beach. There we would play in the sand, and then be joined by my father Yalek. He would hold me in his hands, as I kicked my feet, and taught me to swim. Then he would go for a long swim himself. He would go far out in the ocean. He was a very strong swimmer, a powerful swimmer. I loved to watch him swim.

Yalek was an exceptional young man. He was a mature thinker, a planner, with talent in visual-imagery of architectural drawing and decorating. His parents recognized his intelligence and talents and sent him to Kiev, to the fabricant to learn. After he met Riva and fell in love, he made extensive plans for their life, and including their life with children. He knew that swimming was important for him, he remembered swimming in the Black Sea when he was a boy. That he wanted his children to have a summer home to swim and be healthy. He made the architectural drawings for such a home, with plans for an income property.

At the end of the summer, the first year in Belmar, he found suitable land. It was after the Federal and State Governments had cleared the property rights, and the land of all the wild brush up and down the coast. And after the main highway had been started. He found two lots close to the highway, across the highway, and close to the beach. With a mortgage he bought the land. He already had the architectural plans for the building(s).

The structure he planned and designed was for a building of two apartments, one upper and one down. Each apartment was for four rooms, with bathrooms. Yalek figured to rent the lower floor apartment, for the income, and for his family to live in the second floor apartment. For our family which in the summer included all four children—Little Jack, Big Jack, Freda and myself.

Every summer the four of us children lived in the upper apartment with my mother Riva, and The Babe. On week ends, Ida and Harry came loaded down with food that Ida had prepared.

On Friday night Yalek came after his work, stopping on the way to buy the vegetables and special New Jersey sweet corn and tomatoes. And the special Sweet Cinnamon Bread that we loved, and of course the special deep red Russian flowers for Riva.

Yalek always brought flowers for Riva. He expressed his love this way. He was passionately in love with Riva. And he was very romantic.

Across the front of the building on the second floor, Yalek had built a porch, a covered porch with a roof to protect from the rain. From the porch we could see the ocean and hear the breaking waves, and feel the wet salty spray. At night one could almost touch the stars in the black sky. It was breathtaking, so beautiful. It was Yalek's plan for his children. An outdoor sleeping porch, under the stars and listening to the ocean.

At night Riva and I would open four US Army Cots for the four of us to sleep. We would roll up in blankets, on pillows, and watch the stars, and listen to the ocean waves breaking, and screeching with their own fury, and feel the salt spray on our faces. And sleep the most wonderful sleep anyone can imagine. It was the time for dreaming. I remember these nights sleeping and dreaming with the salt spray in our faces, in our noses.

"Hither and thither on high, the gentle thoughts of the feminine ocean." (Melville)

After Riva's family arrived, the Baba and siblings, and they were living all together on Lamberton Street, it happened that Ida, Riva's younger sister, the extremely talented dress designer, became pregnant with her first child, a boy who they named Jack (after their father Jacob). The father was Harry, Yalek's brother. Harry was Babe Fradle's favorite. He was like her, a heavy set man with the same face as his mother.

It does not need a Delphic oracle to predict what happened. Ida was angry, outraged and felt violated at being made pregnant, by Harry (who she did not love, and barely knew.) The family feeling was also outraged they felt an injustice had been committed.

Thus it happened that two sisters were in relations with two brothers. Big Jack was born amidst this anger and anxiety.

In later years my brother Jack and I have been reminiscing about our father Yalek, recalling that it was he who made these memorable summers possible for us. Sleeping on the open porch every night, watching the bright stars in the black sky, listening to the sounds of the ocean waves breaking with thunder, and feeling the cold spray of the salt water on our faces.

He was an unusual man of intelligence, with talents and skills, and with love and devotion for his wife, Riva, and for us. He saved every penny that he earned to provide for us. He provided a home in the city, and a summer home at the ocean where we could swim in summer and be healthy and strong. And he provided for me my college education, and for Jack, the payment for him to go to school to train as jeweler-watch maker. And for both of us to buy homes for our children.

It was his thoughtfulness in planning for his family since he was a young man and of course his great love and devotion for Riva and his children. Jack and I agree that he loved us and that we loved him. And that we had great respect for him.

CHAPTER III

THE MAN WITHIN MY HEAD

The mind senses those things which it conceives in understanding, as well as those which it has in memory. The eyes of the mind by which it sees things and observes them are proof that it is eternal. THE MAN WITHIN MY HEAD is obviously and without a doubt that of my father Yalek. As I have remembered him for all the years.

It is a composite of all the obsessive memories of him stored in the mind over time, over many years, and in many events. It is a house of built up events, seeing him in different views. And it is the man I finally understood as my father, who he was, that I loved him and that he loved us like he loved Riva.

This is a narrative of stories, of memories, of the history of two families, closely knitted together, closely devoted to each other who grew up in Baranovka, Russia, in early 20th c. It is a story of dreams of individual lives growing up together. I have watched, I have listened to these individuals, who are closely related to me, across the decades to know the effect on their lives. As if someone is peeling off the skin of my own psyche.

I remember when I was young, growing up on Market Street, the first house my father owned. I remember the sheer joy of skating and sledding on the big hills on Broad Street, a main avenue. I loved skating and I was a good skater. I remember coming home about 9 pm to find the door locked. I knew that Yalek locked the door to tell me I was supposed to be home earlier. That was his way of telling me. He did not talk to me generally, or specifically. He was not a talker. He did not know how to talk to us.

I knew about Yalek from the many stories my mother Riva and The Baba told us in the kitchen, evenings, in Yiddish. About the two families, Riva's family and Yalek's family and the legacy they left for us. Yalek and Riva were in love when they were very young, they married young, and soon Yalek left for the US. It was 1905

I was the first grandchild born in this union of the two families. The first child of the most beautiful Riva, and the most handsome Yalek. My mother told how Yalek was so excitedly happy when I was born. He loved me so much. He thought I was beautiful, I looked like Riva with white blond hair and blue eyes. And he worried about taking good care of me. Every day when he came from work he would clean, wet mop the floor under and around my crib, to be sure that there were no dust particles for me to breath.

The air must be spotlessly clean. And the story of when Yakek would go to the union meetings in the evening. He and Riva would go together. He would carry me on his shoulder. He would not leave me at home.

In what seemed to me as a child a short time there were four of us. My parents had my brother Jack, and Ida (and Harry) had (Big) Jack, and then little Freda. It was two sisters joined to two brothers. Thus the families were united, closely knit. closely devoted. We lived close, near each other, as one family, caring for each other.

I was growing up in the heart of this tightly knitted family of young immigrants, where everyone was striving to get educated, to achieve citizenship, and to start a business and to marry.

Yalek was a quiet man who loved his work, as he loved his family. I loved to watch him.

He always rose early. He had a hearty breakfast, usually the left overs of dinner the night before.

Then he went to work. After work he changed into his work clothes and worked on jobs of maintenance. Mostly on the first floor apartment, which was rented. He was very meticulous, very skilled. He knew every kind of construction work needed to build and to maintain a house.

I enjoyed watching him, the way he moved when he worked.

I remember as a child I used to watch Yalek read the newspapers. He loved to read and he loved to know everything about the current news—everywhere. He used to read three daily Yiddish newspapers. When asked about this he said "I need to know what each side is saying."

This was a memory that was with me for many years, for my lifetime. It influenced me, influenced my thinking. To this day I read the daily newspaper and I subscribe and read about ten other publications per month. I need to know what each side is saying, as Yalek said.

I admired my father Yalek; I was impressed with his intelligence, the fact that he loved to read.

But there was something else that was intriguing about him that I needed to discover. Both Riva and Yalek came from highly intelligent, highly educated families in Baranovka. But Yalek was not a talker, he was a quiet man. We never had any conversations about personal matters. And I remember that there were few conversations with my mother Riva.

I never heard words of affection, or words of love between them. In fact I never heard much conversation between them. The atmosphere was most reserved. It was quiet.

I always wondered what happened to him as a child that would cause this lack of talking. It was almost like a fear. I was particularly concerned that I never heard conversation between them, or even signs of affection shown. And there was one recurring image I remember. Every morning I watched as he rolled up the pillow in the blanket and carried it from the living room (where he must have slept) to the bedroom. This was a disturbing memory. As I have thought about my father Yalek all the years this memory is lasting.

I remember well the stories in the kitchen that my mother Riva told about Yalek and the cruelty of his mother Babe Fradle. And I remember how Riva cried when she told this story. She was in pain at the thought of what happened to Yalek., her love.

Babe Fradle managed the big farm, with help of the children. She was an intelligent woman, a authoritarian personality, who was very strict with the children, who had a short temper. She relied on Yalek for most of the help, when she was not pleased she would beat him with a strap.

And send him to sleep in the chicken coops. She did not treat Harry, the second son this way. She favored him. It was thought that it was because he looked just like her—heavy set, with big deep blue eyes. He resembled her in looks, but he was lazy.

I have been looking for meaning, for understanding of my father. Knowing that Yalek was an intelligent man, that he knew he had difficulty talking. But knowing it was difficult to help himself. In those days help was not available.

I remembered Captain Ahab, Moby Dick, who obsessively pursued the white whale.

(Melville, Ch.132, "The Symphony")

> Hither and thither on high glided the snow white wings of
> small unspeckled birds;
> These were the gentle thoughts of feminine air; but to and
> fro in the depths,

> Far down in the bottomless blue, rushed mighty
> Leviathans, swordfish and sharks.
> And these were the strong, troubled, murderous thinkings
> of the masculine sea."

The gentle people of the feminine air were Riva and her devoted family. And then there were The Leviathans, "the troubled murderous thinkings". These were the Babe Fradle—the strong, the angry, her temper, and her beating of Yalek. They seemed to be two contrasting qualities.

I remember watching my father Yalek since I was a very young child. He has been the man within my head, the man I most wanted to know about, the man I wanted to understand. I have thought about him again, and again, as I watched him work so gracefully on the jobs around the house, the maintenance of the roof, the plumbing, the outside porches, and the yards. And I have admired how he worked, how he walked, and how beautifully he swam.

I identified with my father Yalek. I felt that I was most like him, that I had inherited his looks, except those I got from my mother Riva. But I did inherit his intelligence, and his exceptional talent. I knew when I was young that I inherited his talent for design—that I had the eye-hand coordination ability/skill that he had, for decorating, for architecture, for landscaping, and for gardening. For everything I did.

I knew also that the particular eye-hand coordination skill that he had was much like the skill that Ida had for designing and making garments. Although I did not know Yalek very well, we did not talk much. I felt that he recognized in me the same qualities, the similar skills and talents that he had. I wanted to know him. I needed to know him to know myself. And it is possible that he sensed this closeness, and noted the resemblance. I sensed this.

Left: Jane, Jonathan and Yalek
Right: Jane, Bernie, Jonathan, and Yalek

CHAPTER IV

A TOWER OF MEMORIES—THE LOVED ONES

I have lived a long life, a busy life, married to my beloved Bern. A happy life.

It was an arranged marriage, arranged by Bern's father Isaac. It happened at a depressed time, a time of extreme sadness and grief for our small devoted family. It was just after the death of Ida, my Aunt, my mothers sister. They were closely knit, she was my idol.

Bern was much like his father Isaac, a most extraordinary man, indeed a beautiful human being. A man unparalleled (Shakespeare), a man of exceptional intelligence, with superb sense of humor and wit, and handsome beyond many. He was a caregiver of the utmost loving caring. And he had the gift of perfect language.

He made things possible for us, for me and our children, in the quality of life. We all benefited from advanced education, with advanced degrees. And for us to achieve in our professions. And to travel to see the world with vacations in Greece, on the Isle of Mytilene. The isle that used to be called Sappho, after the Greek poet But time passes and now there are only memories to keep alive.

But the memories are fragile and disappear. And finally, my son Jonathan that extraordinary young man, so like his father, in gifted intelligence and talent who is no longer here. He died young of cancer at 59. It is just my elegy to the void, in a place of weeping under a small black headstone.

It was as Czeslaw Milosz said, "More clever than you. I learned my century.

Pretending I knew a method for forgetting pain." But that is impossible.

There is no day, no night, no moment when I do not see him my child. The sorrow remains.

There is no place for my dreams.

My thoughts are focused on remembering my father Yalek, and the sad stories of him, as told by my mother Riva, and her mother Babe Bella, in Yiddish in the kitchen, evenings.

All the years growing up I remember watching my father Yalek. He was always working at jobs of maintenance of his house, and the summer house. He was knowledgeable and skilled. He knew every kind of work necessary to design and build the houses. I admired his knowledge and his skills. But mostly I was awed by his many talents, and his intelligence. And I always hoped that I had inherited some of his talents and abilities, I wanted to identify with him.

In early Spring, I am sitting on a bench on the boardwalk in Belmar with my brother Jack watching that wonderful, magnificent white breaking, roaring ocean that we both love so much.

Jack and I are reminiscing. We both remember growing up with Yalek, and we want to understand our father. Particularly we need to understand why he was so inarticulate for most of our lives growing up with him. And we believe that this was the result of his being beaten by his mother Babe Fradle all those years. And of being sent to sleep in the chicken coops.

But, we do not know enough about his childhood, or why Babe Fradle beat him, rather than Harry her next son. And we do not know enough about Babe Fradle herself as a personality, and psychology, her needs. Or her relationship with Aaron, her husband, to allow such anger and temper. And abuse of her child?

To understand why Yalek, this intelligent, proud man did not talk about himself and his feelings. We think it was because he was not able to talk. It must have been because of events of childhood buried deep within him. He was too proud. In observing his own parents and their dysfunctional relationship he was too affected, too hurt. He never observed his parents say words of love, or never saw them show affection. He never learned to speak of love, with feelings, to have conversations of feelings. He did not know how to talk to us.

Jack and I agreed that we knew our father as a loving person. We know that he was in love with Riva, passionately since they were young. And he loved us. And we loved him and admired him, what a generous loving father he was. Knowing Yalek as we do, Jack and I believe that Yalek knew that he was not a talker, that he was inarticulate, that he had a temper like his mother Babe Fradle, and that he could not control this. He could not forget the pain.

We knew how much we loved him, and we appreciated him. He was a very good father. A man who spent his life for his loved ones. We have loving memories of Yalek.

Remembering the Ocean

> Now small fowls flew screaming over the yet yawning gulf; a sullen white surf beat against its steep sides; then all collapsed, and the great shroud of the sea rolled on as it rolled five thousand years ago.
> —Herman Melville, *Moby Dick*

With pure joy, I remember the gentle thoughts of that ocean every morning. I remember well the early morning swims with my father at six. They were very special. I remember the early morning sun as it rose in the east across the water—how it sparkled so brightly across the entire width of the ocean. The surface literally quivered with brightness.

Every morning, Yalek and I walked across the highway to the ocean edge. It was cold, so we entered the water slowly. Soon we were in the water and swimming. I followed after him. He was a powerful swimmer, slow and strong, and it was hard to keep up. I loved the feel of the cold water around my body with my legs pushing hard against the current. It was the most refreshing feeling, the power of it and the tingling skin from the cold. It was the high point of every day.

Indeed Yalek and I did swim far out against the strong current and the blustery, raging waves. These early morning swims were the only time we spent together. It made the summers for me in Belmar special. We had no other time to talk; he was always busy working or repairing something. It became, for me, a joyous, obsessive memory through the years.

Many years later, while my children were growing up, I taught Jonathan to swim the way Yalek taught me to swim—holding me in his hands. I remember Jonathan saying, "Mom, don't forget I am an ocean baby, just like you and grandpa Yalek." These are words that continue to ring true.

[Section break]

In early spring, on a cold, bright, sunny day in March; my brother, Jack, and I, both now in our nineties, are sitting on a bench on the boardwalk in Belmar, watching the ocean we love. We still love. We watch the waves churn and spray the wet air across our faces, breathing in the salty air. This feeling is very familiar after so many years. We reminisce about when we were children—those wonderful years, growing up here with our parents, Riva and Yalek. They cared for us, watched over us, and gave us the best food. We had fresh fish every day, prepared by Baba Bella. And we had the best swimming experience a child could ever imagine. We know it was these early years that brought us to love the ocean and made us strong swimmers, like Yalek taught us.

Chekhov once said, "Every person lives his real most interesting life under the cover of secrecy." My secret love has always been the ocean. It was my first love. My romance with the ocean began when I was about two, and my father held me in his two hands, and I kicked my feet as he taught me to swim. Every night, as my eyes are closing, my mind reverts to the feeling of the cool water around me. I feel the motion of the perpetually restless waves as they encircle me. I can feel the soft foam of the white waves in my mouth. It is the ocean, with its sensual landscapes, its dark images, and its sounds—like the symbols of an orchestra—that hold the mysteries of the world for me. For me, to read Melville's account of "the feminine ocean," and the "the murderous thinkings of the masculine sea," is to remember my happiest years, growing up in Belmar, at the ocean.

[Section break]

We went to the ocean every weekend so Yalek could work on the bungalows he had built. These became rentals for the summer months. This extra income that he saved for us was for our educations and our houses. All the while, we could swim in the great ocean and have fun growing up.

Bern, my beloved, and I were married more than sixty years ago. It was a marriage arranged by his father, Isaac.

We met at the ocean after the funeral for my Aunt Ida. Ida died unexpectedly of cancer at age forty. Ida and my mother were devoted sisters, almost like twins. As I mentioned earlier, at age eighteen, she immigrated with Riva. She was a skilled dress designer and maker, a talented decorator, and a gifted gardener. She landed a job as an assistant designer of expensive women's blouses. There she met Lisa Maslow, Bern's mother, who also worked there, who introduced her to Isaac, his father.

They became friends with my parents as well. On the Jewish holidays every year, they came to stay with us in our house in Belmar. It was usually toward the end of September, after the summer rental tenants had gone. Isaac was close to Ida; he loved and had great respect for her and her talent. He was most upset and distressed by her sudden death. He came to the funeral; he saw us, her family, consumed with sorrow and grief. As Dr. Samuel Johnson said, "But for sorrow there is no remedy . . . ."

Isaac saw me at the funeral. That was the first time he saw me as an adult. Isaac went home to talk to his son Bern, who later told me his dad had said, "I want you to come with us to Belmar to meet her. She is pretty; she is educated; she comes from a good family."

Bern never said no to his father, so he drove his parents in his car to Belmar to meet me.

As he stepped out of the car, I saw this handsome young man with curly dark hair. He walked up to me, and I saw those exquisite, deep-set, sparkling blue eyes. He saw a pretty young girl with strong, tanned body and light blonde hair. I was wearing handmade, dark-green wool shorts with a halter made from a red bandanna handkerchief.

It was love for both of us. That evening we went for a walk on the boardwalk with the salt spray blowing in our faces. He held my hand tightly. It was forever. We were married soon after and held hands for more than sixty years. We had two children, exceptionally bright and talented—a daughter, Jane, a law professor, and a son, Jonathan, a naturalist, a journalist, and a brilliant writer. He died at age fifty-nine of cancer.

IDA

When I was a teenager, my thoughts were mostly of sewing my own dresses or learning to sew. Living with Ida, my mother's sister and a dress designer, I wanted to be a designer.

> We have yet to discover ourselves. The process of discovery is splendid. It liberates the sacred human person. There is a consciousness that rises independent, calm like the stars. It is the thought of identity—yours for you, as mine for me. Miracle of miracles. It alone has value. Identity, knowing me. The answer is close by.
>
> —Walt Whitman

Ida was my mentor, my muse. She was my idol, my second mother. My aunt Ida was dearest to me; she was my inspiration to become the person I am, with the talents I have in designing, painting, landscaping, gardening, and decorating.

It did not take me long to grow up. It was a focused effort. We would look at the pictures of the newest fashions from Paris. I watched as she translated the image of the dress in her mind, transferring it to the hand that sketched the pattern on the silk material stretched across the dining room table. Everything happened on the dining room table after dinner was served and cleaned up.

I needed to know how to make this transfer—eye to hand—to sketch the pattern, to know that the pieces fit together to form a garment, and to make sure the garment had the right measurements. I was growing up; I needed clothes, in case I might have a date. Buying clothes was out of the question. There was money for the mortgage and money for food—no money for clothes.

I remember the early years, growing up embedded in this tightly woven family of young immigrants striving to work and live together and take care of each other. We all lived closely, dependent on one another.

I remember all those years growing up with Ida as my second mother. I lived with her for most of the time. It was as if I was plastered to her. I was entirely focused on being like her and knowing how to design and make my own clothes.

From the time I was about seven, I hung around the sewing machine. I learned how to sew by hand. I did all the basting and finishing on the dresses and suits she made. I went with her several times a year to Wanamaker's store in New York to buy fabrics—mostly silks that were on sale. By the time I was a teenager, I knew almost everything about designing, except how to use the crayon to draw the garment on the material spread out on the table.

When I graduated from college and was ready to leave home, I was still not sure that I could afford it.

Every morning, Yalek left two dollars on the kitchen table for my mother Riva to buy food for the family. Riva knew how to be frugal. She had grown up in a family of six children with a modest income. So she knew how to manage on little money. She was a superb cook; she knew all about nutrition. The immigrants knew the value of growing and harvesting their own vegetables.

I didn't think about vegetables though. I was a young girl, a teenager, and clothes were what I needed and what I thought about. I knew my family did not have money for clothes for me, or for anyone. Those were difficult times.

By this time, Ida and Harry and their two young children, Big Jack and Freda, and had moved to New Brunswick, New Jersey. They had taken over the grocery store that Sam, Riva's youngest brother, had started. Recently, he had been in an accident when he was on his way home late one rainy Saturday night and his car failed. He was standing in the road, asking for a lift, when he was run down and killed by a drunk driver, a student at Princeton. It was the first, but not the only loss for this young family.

Harry was successful in this new business. The grocery store catered to a special group of people who bought supplies for making whiskey. It was in the Hungarian neighborhod. Most of the customers were bootleggers who lived on farms on the outskirts of the town. Harry fit in perfectly. He became good friends with the bootleggers. They were the same kind. He loved to eat with them and play cards with them. And they loved him. They did not have to come in for their purchases. Harry employed a driver, Gus, especially for them. He was the driver who delivered their orders. Harry was making a great deal of money—all in cash. When he took a nap on the sofa, and he was a large man, the money would fall out of his pockets. As children, we laughed. We did not know how Ida siphoned off the money for the rest of the family.

On Sunday, after a big dinner that Ida always made, I would clear the table completely. Ida would spread the silk material on the table pad then, with a wax crayon, she would draw the pattern of the dress. Then she would pin together the parts and stitch them on the sewing machine. When the dress was ready for finishing, it was ready for me. I did the hand finishing and then the hemming.

The actual operations, the cutting and sewing, seemed short; it was the waiting for Ida that seemed endless. And it could take a long time to get a finished garment. So I waited. I had no choice, but I was determined that I would do whatever was needed. The process was long. Ida's time was short. She was raising a family, a working mother, and helping Harry in the store.

Ida worked, the children went to school, and I went to school with no wardrobe. Oh, yes, Ida bought me a coat and gave my mother the money for shoes. I had two pairs of underwear. Baba Bella came every day to look for clothing for Sara's children. Sara's husband, Sam, was a great reader. He read every book in the library, but he had no job, no trade, He could not make a living for his family. They depended on Ida

Every day, Baba Bella took one pair of underwear from my drawer for Sara. That left me with one pair of underwear. When I asked, "How do I manage with one pair?" she replied, "You'll manage."

To describe my wardrobe as slim would be to misuse the word, a great understatement.

I desperately needed to learn. I wanted to design and make my clothes, to know how to make the pattern, to cut and sew. I already knew how to do all the handwork and finish the garment.

I don't think anyone in the world around me was aware of my enormous desire. In fact, I don't think anyone in my family knew me or knew anything about my obsessive ambition to be a designer. I knew of no other way of having a wardrobe of clothes that consisted of more than one of each thing. I lived with Ida and Harry and the children in their home during the four years I attended college in New Brunswick. And every day I thought about my obsessive desire to design and make my own clothes. The more I worked at completing my plan, the better I got at figuring out each step. I continued to plan and work at my dressmaking skills.

Each garment I worked on improved my hand-eye coordination, which was necessary to design, cut, and sew the dress together. With each garment, I was getting better; I could design in my head and figure out the form and the pattern shape. I needed to mark out the pattern with my eyes, to draw it, then cut, and finally fit. It was exacting work—the pieces cut needed to fit together. I was determined to learn. I was strongly motivated. I needed clothes.

After Bern and I married and I was at home for a few years with our young children, Freda met Elliot; mutual friends introduced them. Soon they decided to marry. Because I was so close to Freda, having raised her with Riva's help, we planned the wedding. I decided that I would make her engagement dress and the dress for her wedding. That brought me back to the sewing machine. I have the picture of the young beautiful Freda in the beautiful dress I made for her engagement.

It was after Freda's marriage to Eliot that I began to design children's dresses. I was stimulated by my own need for my own child. I began making designs for independent contractors of expensive children's dresses. And several years later, I began to design ladies' blouses made of silk and linen. These were not the ordinary styles; they were silk blouses with detailed handwork. Over time, I produced hundreds of original ladies' blouses in silk or linen, with much detailed handwork.

After many years of practice in designing and making these beautiful garments, I had mastered the hand-eye coordination needed to get the patterns and measurements correct and to produce perfectly fitting, handsomely made garments.

I often dream of the designs I still want to make—of the curtains and bedspreads I want to create from the beautiful fabrics I have, of the flowers I want to plant, and of the beautiful clothes I want to make for my granddaughter, Emily, and for my great-granddaughter, the beautiful baby Talya.

Jonathan E. Maslow (1948-2008), a Wondrous Son

This man believed that every human has the duty to love and assist every other human because that is all we have. And this is what the Anglos call a radical, a communist, and worse.

—Jonathan Maslow, *The Torrid Zone*

(His) laugh was the loudest, the most majestic sound, as if needing a respite from the gravity of every day living. What is poetry which does not save nations or people.

—Ceslaw Milosz

Jonathan Maslow was an extraordinary man, a brilliant man, a man without parallel. He was an accomplished writer, a journalist, a documentary filmmaker, and a committed environmentalist. He published six books by an early age. He was a writer blessed with three remarkable gifts; he was a thinker of genuine originality, a reader of astonishing erudition, and a writer of breathtaking prose. He was also a poet. (See poems, *Skulls*, with woodcuts by Leonard Baskin. See also *A Prayer for the City*.)

He was born a most beautiful, most happy child, who fell in love with nature. He was a naturalist, the embodiment of Charles Darwin, from the time he was four years old, walking with me and the two dogs in the woods behind our house. On these walks, he learned the names of the trees, the plants, the birds, and the flowers. He learned on his own how to rescue the ducks that wintered in the swamp, the wetlands in our woods, when they were injured.

Jonathan was raised on words, words, and words from the time he was born. He inherited a keen musical ear from his dad, Bern, and he spoke perfect English. Bern had great linguistic ability with excellent English syntax. He had a gifted language ability for speaking and writing.

Jonathan grew up listening to stories in the kitchen, stories told by my mother, Riva, and grandma, Baba, in Yiddish. By the time he was in high school, he was a wordsmith with exquisite language. He was also a ferocious reader, and he knew that he wanted to be a writer and a naturalist early in his life. He had already met the owl that seduced him when he was about ten. I found this owl sitting on the limb of a tree outside Jonathan's bedroom window. This little owl was the passion of his life. He wanted to learn about owls and birds when he was in high school, so he went to Columbia University for two courses, Ornithology and Anthropology.

His first book was about owls, *The Owl Papers*. The second book was also about birds, the quetzal bird and the unsavory politics of Guatemala. It was titled *Bird of Life, Bird of Death*.

Philip Roth, his friend and mentor, said he admired Jonathan's tremendous intellect. He said, "He was brilliant, and with his range as a writer, he could do newspaper work, a naturalist book, a travel piece, or a thought piece. He was phenomenally capable and talented as a writer."

His voice was fueled by endlessly stretching the imagination of the people he wrote for and providing joy from his often wild sense of humor. For this he was always well prepared with plentiful stories he remembered from his childhood of listening at the kitchen table. He was a poet writing with a free spirit, a reprise of Walt Whitman. His prose was mellifluous. (See *The Torrid Zone*.)

In the proposal for his column, "A Bend in the River" (the *Herald News*), Jonathan wrote,

> I believe in my soul that a writer's contribution to the world is made by scribbling the universal script as it plays out in one particular place. And mine, for better or worse, is in New Jersey, particularly at the shore among the wetlands, which I have loved.

"Let ordinary people see themselves in the stories you print," was the advice Jonathan, the editor, gave to his reporters.

> When something happens in your coverage area, ask the common people. The readers cannot take a newspaper's opinion 100 percent about government and politics anymore than they can live by eating only carrots.

He encouraged writers to write human stories about individuals experiencing tragedy and overcoming tragedy, showing courage, living life as it is. This was the honest democratic journalism Jonathan believed in. Journalists have been put on this earth by the Creator to protect us and protect our democracy.

Jonathan was the first western journalist to report from the Central Asian country Turkmenistan in the late nineteen eighties. He covered civil wars in Central America in the seventies and eighties. He made four documentary films; he wrote six books and won fellowships as a journalist while working in Russia, Central Asia, and Guyana. "I like to go to beautiful places with big problems."

Jonathan's life was his writing. He was not just searching out writing as a life, but writing as art for a real life. His writing was at the core of his humanity. His writing sensibilities were kindred to William Blake's romanticism and Walt Whitman's vision as a rebel.

Jonathan believed that a strange, painful division between a person and a society gets covered up with memories. He believed that writing truth was needed to reaffirm this reality. Being creative and seeking ways to make this the basis of social life was the answer—that writing was the most complete version of the human effort to make this effective in the public realm. Wallace Stevens once wrote, "The world is ugly, and the people are sad."

I try to recall Jonathan's voice. I feel the need to sit and touch the earth near the small, black headstone where he lies. His words, his beautiful language, his poetry has returned.

> "A place weeping enters our sleep," wrote the Kurdish poet
> Bejan Matur, never leaves.
>
> Nothing but land swept earth, nothing but silence
>
> His words, however are audible to our ears and
>
> We can repeat them and go on doing so
>
> The first movement is singing, a free voice filling
> mountains and valleys
> The first movement is joy, but it is taken away
> What is poetry which does not save nations or people
> What is the use of magic that doesn't assuage despair

What attracted me to his poetry? The language. I fell in love with the freedom with which he respected and defied the rules. He was never doctrinaire. There was a constant energy in his writing.

> Day after day, I think of you as I wake up.
> Someone has put the cries of birds
> On the air like jewels.
>   (Vallejo)a

An Extraordinary Man: Bernard Maslow

At rare intervals there appears among us an individual whose extraordinary qualities are so outstanding that he is always remembered. That man was my husband of sixty years, Bernard Maslow, a man of extraordinary intelligence, profound wisdom and understanding, and an exceptional sense of humor and wit combined with great compassion for all human beings. He had a selfless generosity of spirit. He was generous beyond everyone. He lived his life devoted to his loved ones. He was like his dad, Isaac, in every respect—in looks and in character and in his relations with people.

Bern's father, Isaac, arranged my marriage. It was after my aunt Ida died so unexpectedly at age forty. Isaac was a very good friend. He had known Ida since she had arrived in New York at age eighteen. He came to her funeral to grieve with this utmost mourning family of immigrants. She was an exceptional woman, a talented woman, a woman of intelligence and culture. She was a remarkable woman, exceptionally talented dress designer. She died too soon of breast cancer.

When he returned home, he spoke to Bern. He said, "I would like you to come with us to visit the family and to meet this young woman. She is pretty; she is educated. And she needs someone to take care of her."

Of course, Bern would never say no to Isaac. That was July. In late September, Isaac and Lisa usually came to the Jersey Shore for a long weekend during the Jewish holidays. This time, Bern drove them in his car. They got out of the car. He saw me playing ball with the younger children, saw my head of blonde hair and my figure, suntanned, wearing dark-green wool shorts that I had made and a red bandanna handkerchief as halter top. I looked like a farm girl. He had grown up in New York City, and his friends were city girls, perhaps more sophisticated.

Bern fell in love as soon as he saw my blonde hair. I saw this handsome young man, who looked like Isaac, with curly black hair and piercing sapphire-blue eyes. He was so serious, so knowing. I knew that I loved him even before we met. I had dreamed of him, needed him. That evening, as we walked on the boardwalk, he held my hand tightly in his. We were feeling the salt spray on our faces. He held my hand in his tightly for the rest of our lives. We fell in love with the cold wet spray in our faces. We listened to the crashing waves roar as they struck the beach.

It was in this magical throbbing ocean landscape that we met and fell in love. Our love was forged in this ocean. Our two children were born here at the ocean. This was the ocean I have loved since my childhood.

Bern was a quiet man, a serious man, and a gentle man, always warm and giving. He had an exceptional sense of humor with sharp, unforgettable wit and sparkling blue eyes. He was the mirror image of Isaac, with a broad handsome face, wonderful white hair, and a fierce intellect. And like Isaac, he loved people. He was extremely generous. He cared about people.

Bern was a rare individual with a highly gifted mind. He was informed about the world and about politics. As a young boy, he was always seeking to know everything—a prodigious reader. He wanted to know. He questioned.

"The problem was to acquire the knowledge of life that goes beyond the ordinary, the mundane," Camus wrote. Bern wanted to know about all issues. He was erudite, intelligent, and profoundly thoughtful.

When he was five years old, his mother took him and his sister, who was three years older, to take piano lessons. The teacher said he was a talented child who was gifted musically and had a love of music.

As he grew older, he loved listening to classical music, and he especially loved the opera. He listened faithfully on Saturday and Sunday to the New York Philharmonic Symphony and the Metropolitan Opera performances. This love of cultural activities was an important part of daily life for him as a child, and it became a part of our lives with our children.

When the children were growing up, Bern made sure that we attended concerts and the ballet, which was also a favorite of his. He also enjoyed going to museums and seeing all the special exhibits. Reading was a necessity for him; he was a fast and thorough reader. Our children were the same. This was his gift, he made it possible for his family to absorb the same culture he had shared with his dad, Isaac. He made it possible for us to have these interests.

In the midsixties, while working in the public school system as speech therapist, I developed a program to improve the kindergarten, first grade, and second grade curriculums for reading. This was a pilot demonstration I conducted every week for six classes of children. I conducted this program for seven years, and the reading scores, were improved. This was phenomenal. Bern suggested that I should be teaching teachers at the college level. He found the job for me as Professor of Education, Vermont State Colleges. We drove to the interview, and I got the job. He left his job as Director of Plants and Facilities at a high school and arranged our move to Vermont. He made it possible for me to be a professor of education and train teachers at the college level.

At end of the year of teaching college, the professor of reading suggested that I get a doctorate. I was accepted into the program, and in three years I received a doctorate in reading education after three years. Bern made this possible.

Bern was an extraordinary man—an exceptional, caring individual, he made things possible. For him, our life together meant total love and devotion. He loved his family passionately and lived to make everything possible for us that we needed or wanted. He made it possible for each one of us to achieve our career goals. He provided for our daughter, Jane, to go to Wellesley and then Harvard Law School. Jonathan went to Wesleyan and then to Columbia School of Journalism. After that, he went to Central America and on to become a naturalist, a writer, and a journalist.

I could never have made it through to achieve and earn a doctorate degree at the age of fifty-nine without him. He always made the arrangements to make it possible. Bern was a man unparalleled in love and devotion, in selflessness and caretaking. Bern was an extraordinary man, a remarkable man. He loved us passionately.

CHAPTER V

THE NEW WORLD OF GARDENS

THE PALACE OF MEMORIES

Seeing with the eye of a poet I see Yalek arriving in NYC from Baranovka. Russia, with his younger brother Harry. It was 1905. This handsome young man was married to Riva his childhood love in Baranovka. He was coming here to find work, to establish himself and send for Riva.

It was the early 20th c, the time of much emigration of young people from the countries of Eastern Europe, from Russia and Poland, Italy and Ireland. For decades there was economic depression and political oppression over all of Europe. Most of the young people were running away from their own countries to find a better life.

Yalek had no difficulty finding a job as a china decorator at Lenox China, the finest china company located in Trenton, N.J. Yalek found his way there. He rented a room in the working class neighborhood. Harry also found a job. Yalek began saving his money.

By 1910 Yalek had saved enough for passage for Riva and her family, The Baba and the five siblings. Riva's father Jacob had died suddenly in the Flu epidemic the previous year. After Yalek sent the money for passage he looked for a house big enough for all of them. He found a small row—house where they could live.

All the young immigrants, Riva's siblings, began attending school at night. All wanted to apply for citizenship. All were adjusting to the new land quickly learning English, finding partners to marry, working at jobs with their talents, and starting their own businesses. Herman married and started his own business, a new style grocery store. Ben soon married and started his own new grocery store in an ethnic neighborhood. Sara went to school, finished high school and then got her degree as a Chiropractic. Sam, the youngest brother married and started his own new grocery store, in New Brunswick. (NJ) in an ethnic Hungarian neighborhood. It was one hour ride to Trenton where he lived with his new wife and new baby girl.

The new style grocery was where customers bought by the pound; a pound of sugar, pound of flour, pound of rice, pound of coffee, etc It was a development of the times, and it was the populations from the European countries that were familiar with this type of buying groceries in their countries.

The young immigrants had grown up in Baranovka, Russia, the Ukraine region with the most fertile soil in all of Europe. Their food was mostly all home grown.

Yalek and Riva and their siblings were excited about living in New Jersey. New Jersey has been as the Garden State. It was from its beginning known for its corn and tomatoes. These two crops were the best in the country. The soil in NJ is particularly favorable for corn and for tomatoes. I remember as a child hearing about the "Beef Steak Tomatoes" which were so delicious.

Riva and her siblings were especially happy in the summer time when all along the New Jersey highways the Farm stands were open selling home grown fruits and vegetables. And Yalek loved to shop for the vegetables and the tomatoes and corn every week when he came to Belmar. Especially he loved buying the large deep red Russian flowers to bring for Riva.

Soon it was time for the next generation. My generation, Big Jack, Little Jack, Freda and me. It was the family tree sprouting, with the new seedlings. Each one of us a new tree, the same or different species? Who will we be like, whose genes will we inherit? Whose personality?

In many ways we are defined by our families, we carry them within us in our daily lives. In many ways our lives are similar to the people we come from. Who will we be like? This has been for me a constant observation for most of my childhood.

Keeping in mind Babe Fradle who was Yalek's mother, who was known as a severe parent who ruled her children with severe beatings. She was known to beat Yalek, her oldest most intelligent, most talented child. To expel him from the house and make him sleep in the chicken coops. Who will inherit her genes, her personality?

In the history books Baranovka, which is in southwest of Russia, was a town in the core of the fiercest battles of World War II. In the National Holocaust Museum there is a list of the names of all the towns and shtetles that were eliminated in the fierce fighting. Baranovka no longer appears on the map of Russia. It was disappeared.

Jonathan Maslow Naturalist, Writer, Journalist (died of cancer, age 59) traveled to Russia in 1950's to see Baranovka where his ancestors came from. He reported that Baranovka was no longer there. It had been completely destroyed in the War II.

RELIGIOSITY, FOOD

Riva's parents Bella and Jacob grew up and lived in Baranovka, Russia all their lives. Jacob was a talented shoe designer and maker, his shop was attached to the house. He was known as a Jewish intellectual, by nature a "fierce reader" who spent much of his time in the synagogue discussing philosophy with the other Jewish intellectuals of the community. Jacob was a mentor for his children, he liked to discuss philosophy and religion with them. It is from him that the children naturally thought a great deal about the Hebrew orthodox religious way of life and its customs of keeping a "kosher kitchen".

The children all knew the history of the Jews and the reasons for the belief in the orthodox customs. They had many discussions about the customs of Bar Mitzva and the observance of the Jewish Holidays. Being an intelligent parent Jacob did not insist that they adopt the orthodox customs, He thought that they should make the decision for themselves.

Arriving in this country as young people ready soon to get married and set up housekeeping Riva and her siblings thought about their choice. It was the time when many young Jewish intellectuals were re-considering their own growing up in Jewish orthodox homes. And they were thinking what it would mean for their children. It was the time when the new political freedom was being discussed. And it was the time when some young people rejected the Jewish Orthodox life style and instead chose the new "Jewish Atheism".

Listening to their father Jacob, and knowing the history of the Jewish customs, Riva and most of her siblings, rejected the orthodox practices of keeping a "kosher kitchen". Instead they chose to be non-orthodox. Riva and Yalek were already among the new "Jewish Atheists". The others soon followed. Only Ben kept the Orthodox style. He married Celia who wanted their children to be Bar Mitzvah.

Jacob died suddenly in the 1910 flu epidemic. It was just as they were ready to come to the US. The young family was in the midst of total grieving when they arrived. All six children then decided that after they married their first born male child would be named after "Jacob" to honor him. I was the first born grandchild. After me came Ida's child, a boy called Jack. Then followed by Riva's son, my brother Jack. In all, there were four "Jack's" in the family named after Jacob.

After I was born, Yalek bought a two-family house for his family in Trenton. After we were settled he joined a union. In my loving remembrance I see him going to the meetings at night, with Riva and with me on his back, to be sure I was safe.

Yalek was a happy man with his family. He realized his dreams.

After my brother Jack and I were both in elementary school, Yalek enrolled us in the Yiddish Workers School, an after school program similar to the Jewish-Hebrew School where most families sent their children. Jack and I loved this new school. Everything was in Yiddish language. We learned to read and write in Yiddish, we learned the Jewish literary authors, we learned Jewish music and art and dance. We were thoroughly educated in the Yiddish language history and literature. We especially loved reading the work of Sholem Aleichem, His stories and the humor are still memorable for us. We feel richer for knowing the works in Yiddish.

The other siblings of Riva and Yalek. only two, Freda (and Eliot) with three children, and Ben (and Clara) with four children chose to have their children be Bar Mitzvah.

SWEET, SWEET CINNAMON BREAD

Talking to (Dr. McGovern) during my annual check up for my pace-maker, I happened to mention several times that in my mother's house we ate vegetables in summer months by the "bushel", not by the pound. He was fascinated and spent an hour asking me questions. Yalek and Riva, my parents and their siblings grew up in Baranovka, Russia, which was in The Crimea, the richest fertile agricultural land of middle Eastern Europe. The population all had their own large gardens of vegetables and fruit orchards. Most had their own cows, their own wholesome milk. The best cheese and the best sweet cream and sour cream. We grew up on the best diets, the most nutritious foods.

When they emigrated from Baranovka and came to New Jersey they felt very much at home in the Garden State of the nation, known for its fruits and vegetables and especially the "best sweet corn and best tomatoes". Yalek and Riva, and their families knew what to do with fresh produce, they grew up raising their own. I described to him how my mother Riva and Ida used to prepare the vegetables. In our family we loved fresh corn. When the corn was in season it was common for each person to eat at least 4 ears. My father Yalek held the record with 6 ears.

But best of all my brother Jack and I still remember growing up with the wonderful taste of the sweet Cinnamon Bread that Yalek used to bring us every Friday evening when he would come to Belmar after his week of work.

Every Friday after work Yalek bathed and dressed in fresh clothes to come to Belmar. After Trenton the next town is Robbinsville. There was a local bakery that made the most wonderful Cinnamon Bread. Every week he stopped to buy breads for us. Further down the road into the country were the large farms. Here he stopped and bought the vegetables, the corn, tomatoes, peppers, eggplants and squash. A bushel each. Then at the last farm stand the farmers were originally from Russia. They cultivated the large deep red Russian sage flowers. Yalek always brought bunches of these deep red flowers for Riva. He was indeed a romantic man. He never forgot to bring flowers and that wonderful sweet cinnamon bread for his family.

In Israel the Kibbutz Farms was being started. A new style of living based on cooperative living. A large group of people living together farmed the land for food for themselves, and for income, selling their produce to the markets. All the people lived cooperatively. The children were educated in cooperative schools but lived with their families. They all lived as vegetarians.

When Yalek left Baranovka to come to the US, Yalek's two brothers and sister Rachel also left Baranovka, but went instead to Israel. They had been following the development of The Kibbutz and since they were vegetarians themselves they wanted to live in Israel. They lived on a Kibbutz for many years.

Yalek and Riva's diet was mostly vegetarian. They ate little meat, mostly fish and chicken and vegetables. Riva's siblings and their families were also mostly vegetarians. Their love for garden vegetables and their knowledge of nutrition started in the fertile gardens of Baranovka, in the Ukraine.

During the summer when we lived in Belmar, every morning at 6 am The Baba went down to the beach where the fishermen were bringing in their nets filled with the daily catch. She was a very petit, pretty woman. She put her finger to her lips and said, "I'll have one of these and one of these" etc.

She brought home the fish, washed them and put them in the roasting pan with vegetables. We ate like Kings: baked fish with vegetables every day.

All of my childhood experiences in Belmar, loving the rough swimming in the ocean, loving sleeping on the second floor open porch, watching the stars with the salty spray covering our faces, loving eating the fresh fish The Baba made for us every day have been imprinted. And the memories of Yalek bringing us the sweet, sweet Cinnamon Bread on week ends, and bringing the deep red Russian

Sage flowers for Riva are also embedded in deep memory. Also, being able to attend the Yiddish Shule, thanks to our father Yalek and learning to read and write, especially to read Scholem Aleichem in the Yiddish are deep in my memory palace.

They are simply and lovingly arranged with time. A reassuring refuge deep in my memory palace.

A YIDDISH LEGACY

Growing up in our house life centered in the kitchen. Where we listened every evening to stories about Baranovka, told by my mother Riva and The Baba in Yiddish. We were raised on words, words, words, in the manner of Wittgenstein, Words were in the air, tumbling off the table, rolling on the floor. The words were melodies, songs as if someone had written a musical. Our ears became tuned to the sounds of Yiddish. My brother Jack and I, and later my son Jonathan loved listening to the stories.

The stories were told in the kitchen by Riva and The Baba and visitors from the old country Baranovka. The air was crackling with Yiddish words and what passed as English they were learning. As children we were fascinated.

The stories about life in Baranovka, among their families told of a rich life even though the times were sometimes poor. Living in the agricultural region of the Ukraine, where the land was rich, very fertile, they all had gardens which produced all their food.

We are defined by the family stories we carry within us. But, at the same time families are the place where storytelling begins. The first stories we know are the ones we hear from family, about what happened to them. Childhood is the time of stories when everything is possible and every story can still be true.

Growing up listening to stories tolled by Riva and the Baba in the kitchen in Yiddish, we learned about life in Baranovka, a far country, in a foreign tongue. We learned the Yiddish language and began to hear its special melodies and harmonies as well as the diversity of voices and colors. And especially its very wonderful humor. My brother Jack and I learned quickly and we became fluent speakers of Yiddish. We could converse with the older folks accurately as natives. They were pleased. Especially since we could read the Yiddish newspaper.

For our parents Riva and Yalek, listening to their children speaking in Yiddish was a wish fulfilled. Yalek was a highly educated man. His family were known as intellectuals Yalek and his siblings were educated in Hebrew, and Riva and her siblings also were educated in Hebrew in the synagogue school. In those times all Jewish families sent their children to be educated in order to be Bar Mitzvah. But Jacob, Riva's father was an intellect who studied philosophy and history and knew the history of the Jewish people. Being an intelligent man Jacob did not want to influence his children to simply follow the traditional orthodox way. He had faith in their intelligence and knew that they would decide for themselves.

Yalek was educated and he knew the history of the Jewish people. He knew that the Hebrew language had not been used for conversation or for commerce.

It was only used for educating children for Bar Mitzvah. He was a pragmatist, a modernist and understood the history. He knew also that many immigrants coming from countries where the Jewish people had known only the orthodox way would choose to stay with that way. Most Jewish families joined the "Reform Synagogues" that were forming rapidly. But Yalek had strong faith in the language and culture of Yiddish. He believed that it would survive.

Fortunately it was the time in this country when several union worker groups established their own schools for their members' children. After school programs completely in Yiddish. Luckily such a Yiddish Shule school was opened in our city.

Yalek enrolled us.

The curriculum included the history of Judeism and the culture, the reading all Yiddish literature, knowing Yiddish music and theater, and dance. We learned to speak, to read, to write in Yiddish. We were fluent in the language. Especially pleasing to our father Yalek, we learned to read the daily newspaper in Yiddish.

Classical Yiddish writing, the writing of Yiddish stories occurred in three essential movements from 1864 to 1917. These were associated with three names S.T. Abramovitch, the grandfather of modern Yiddish literature, Sholem Aleichem the grandson who raised it to new heights, and I.L. Peretz the "father" of the new literary generation who founded Yiddish modernism. The Yiddish stories of these three main authors look back at Jewish life in Eastern Europe.

Sholem Yankev Abramovich was the central figure in the development of modern Yiddish fiction. He was the first writer to produce Yiddish novels on a par with nineteenth century fiction in other languages. Sholem Aleichem followed his mentor's works but continued the satiric bent, He moved toward a popular humoristic style. He showed Yiddish readers Tevye's ability to "laugh through tears". Isaac Peretz influenced Yiddish fiction by introducing a compressed style and avante-guard techniques.

These classic Yiddish authors' main goal in writing their stories with humor was to help reform the Jewish communities through their social criticism. The early Jewish writers began writing their stories in Hebrew but switched to Yiddish in the 1860's. It was because as one writer said "Most of our people don't even know Hebrew. They speak only Yiddish. Hebrew lacked the everyday vocabulary to represent everyday life in Eastern Europe. Besides the Jewish writers found it difficult to describe the people in shtetl life in the Hebrew language. Like the Jewish beggars.

Sholem Aleichem, the best of the Yiddish writers was most successful in representing Yiddish life, in describing their sense of humor as misfortune befalls them. Sholem Aleichem was known as one of the greatest comic authors in Yiddish.

The reforms of the 1860's allowed the Jews to study in Russian language schools and private elementary schools, and in the universities. Sholem Aleichem benefitted from the reforms under Alexander II. He was then able to study in a Russian high school. He was well educated in Russian literature which influenced his later Yiddish writing.

Both Jack and I have happy remembrances going to the Jewish Shule every week when we were growing up and learning to read in Yiddish. We first learned of the stories of Sholem Aleichem in the shule and discovered Yiddish humor as the funniest we ever heard. We always laughed till we cried when reading the stories.

Sholem Aleichem's writing was the so-called "realistic" writing of the time. It closely resembled the writing of Chekhov for its concentration and economy of expression. At the same time it was his own style of broad flowing, and detailed explanations. Chekhov was very fastidious about "humor". He had little patience for the current crop of Russian writers who writing in the Yiddish press. They thought they were humorists.

Sholem Aleichem was the only Jewish writer who came in close contact with all levels of his people. He wanted to know them as if they were his close relatives. His extraordinary literary popularity was due most of all to his great simplicity of expression.

He had an open curious character. The multifaceted group of Jews that moves through his works was not an odd group that he adopted. It was his own world in which he felt himself at home and moved around freely. He had personal acquaintance with and connections to everyone, the rich factory owner or the lowly garbage man.

And the poor "goldspinners", and Berke the bathhouse attendant, and Tevye the dairyman and his rich son-in law. All of them held deep human interest for him. That determined his style, the way he wrote about them.

Was Sholem Aleichem more drawn to the "highest" or to the "lowest" level of society?

Inwardly he was wholeheartedly rooted with "simple Jews". To him they were the" real Jews." To him the "simple folk" was synonymous with "honest folk". The segment of the people who hold within themselves the honest simplicity of generations. In contrast he rejected no class of people, the "aristocrats" which he thought of as a withered branch of a tree—the people.

I believe that to Jack and to me we could feel the connection that Sholem Aleichem was making with how he described his characters, It reflected what we had been hearing and learning growing up in our Yiddish home. It was as if he was in our kitchen talking like Riva and The Baba. It was the same language. The same as in our heads.

Jack and I grew up in a family where Yiddish was the primary language spoken even though they were all learning English as fast as they could. We were the children of secular Jews for whom the Hebrew language meant no more than any other foreign language. Our parents Yalek and Riva, and their family The Baba and siblings were educated in a Yiddish culture in Baranovka. And when Yalek learned of the Yiddish Worker Schools he and Riva were happy. He knew that this is what they wanted for us.

We were a very closely knit family, very devoted to each other. A tight-knit family for whom the Yiddish culture was important and natural. We grew up listening to stories, listening to music, and reading the literature and the newspapers. It was both religion and culture. We were a family primarily. We all loved the culture of music and art, and we all loved reading the literature. We considered going to the Yiddish Schule a privilege.

Bernie and Clara

Bernie, Bouvier 2, and Clara   Clara and Bouvier 2

CHAPTER VI
THE LEGACY OF STORIES

I remember listening to the stories told by my mother and Baba every evening in the kitchen—stories of their family, of Jacob, of Baba Bella, of their children, and of the love and devotion among them. I also remember the stories about Yalek growing up in his family with his mother, Babe Fradle, and Aaron and siblings.

I remember the utter joy of the early morning ocean swims with my father as we entered the cold water, facing east, as the early morning sun rose with pulsating brilliance—an image I can never forget. And I remember the stories of how Riva was in love with Yalek when they were very young.

I remember the stories of these families as immigrants, where every day, something would occur of major significance—where every day, Riva and her sister Ida were on a rescue mission. Some days, it was just a need for money for food or children's clothing or school. Mostly it was for Sara, their sister in need. She was married to Sam, a great reader; he read every book in the library. But he could not make a living. On other days, it was truly crisis management.

I often find myself replicating recipes, just as Ida did or Riva did. And I garden as Ida did her garden, producing similar flowers. And surely, in my own friendships over the years, I have been friendly with people, like Riva and Ida were. I love people, as I saw they did.

And I knew these things about Ida and Riva not only through what I observed, but also through the stories they told.

In many ways we are defined by our family stories. We carry these stories with us all our lives. Our lifestyles, our cultural traits, are replicas of our legacy of stories. They determine who we are.

For me, these stories begin with the two prominent families in Baranovka and end with the lives of the third generation in this country. They create a special book of memories.

This started as a book of stories of obsessive memories of Yalek and his life in Baranovka. They begin with the hub of darkness with Babe Fradle and her harsh treatment of him and end in the light of happiness of the second generation, which includes Jonathan, a wondrous, extraordinary child.

The death of Big Jack, the second-born grandchild, son of Ida and Harry, is a final sorrow. Big Jack was a brilliant child who excelled in school; he went to MIT and then to work as an engineer at the Princeton Institute of Science, where he worked with Jon von Neumann, the mathematician, on the A-bomb. While at Princeton, he was friendly with Albert Einstein.

Born into a world where nature is indifferent to our desires and our aspirations, we struggle to find our place in it. We are shaped, molded, and influenced by our backgrounds—by one or more of our ancestors. Listening to the stories about our family in the old country, I hoped I would learn about the individuals as people. I wanted to know how they loved and how they expressed love because that was something that wasn't in the stories I heard.

I know that my father, Yalek, loved my mother, Riva. They had loved each other in Baranovka since they had been young. I know that they loved each other passionately; I heard this from Riva. Yet there was never any love shown as we were growing up. In the telling of the stories, I was looking for personality traits and meaning.

Having chronicled the stories of Yalek—of the beatings by his mother Babe Fradle—when he was young, and knowing of his inability to talk to us of personal things, I wonder what will happen with the next generation? And with generations to come?

My brother was working at Fort Monmouth, in the US Army Signal Corps, as a technician, when he met and fell in love with Sophie, a pretty young woman from the neighboring town of Long Branch. After serving in the US Army for his two-year service he returned to find her. Sophie and Jack were married. They had two daughters. With help from Yalek, they purchased a large house in a suburban neighborhood.

Sophie had four siblings. Sophie's mother, Philomena, was divorced from her husband. She owned a grocery store in a neighborhood largely populated by black people and Jews. She was strongly opinionated and bigoted and had old-world, Italian beliefs. Her children were also known to have these opinions.

Freda and I lived near Jack for several years. However, we did not know about Jack and Sophie's relationship with their daughters, assuming everything to be normal. We did not know that Jack was having difficulty. When their daughters were in high school, Sophie routinely made fun of Jack by criticizing his poor syntax. This was humiliating for my brother. He was hurt but could not refute. His way of handling the situation was to walk to the next room and cry. The children laughed along with their mother. This humiliation lasted many years.

After Sophie's death, Jack met a woman in the therapy group who was very different. She respected him, loved him, and treated him with care.

In the case of my cousin, Big Jack, he was raised differently than I was. He was born to Ida when she was only nineteen. Her life was turned by the unexpected motherhood.

When Jack was five months old, Ida took him to New York to see her friends Lisa and Isaac. She thought she could care for him herself while she worked at her new job in New York's garment district. Her friends Lisa and Isaac could not help her. She returned to the family.

Finally, it was revealed that Yalek's brother Harry was the father. Soon after, Ida and Harry moved to New Brunswick. Harry had been given the grocery store that Sam had started.

Jack was an unusually beautiful child; he had Harry's round face and penetrating dark eyes, He resembled Harry's mother Babe Fradle. He was very intelligent. When he attended school, he was above average in all subjects and brilliant in mathematics. Our aunt Sara, Riva's youngest sister, recognized his intellect early on and called him "a genius."

Harry did not know how to be a father. He spoiled them, just as Babe Fradle spoiled Harry. Gus, the grocery-store driver, drove Jack to school, which was only a few blocks from home. He did not walk to school like the other neighboring children—he was chauffeured. He was the center of Ida and Harry's world. Everyone was his subordinate. He was the smartest and always knew the right answer.

Jack was developing into a narcissist early on. Among the relatives, he was different. In his personal life, he had few friends. He had serious problems developing a social life and had difficulty with interpersonal relationships. This seems to be the legacy from two generations descended from Babe Fradle, a petty, tyrannical person, who prioritized superiority and the need to be better and smarter than everyone.

From Harry, Big Jack learned to focus on himself, on feeling good, on eating what he liked, on doing what he liked, and on listening to loud music. Harry did not know of devotion, of being devoted to someone—his family, his children. Big Jack was happy to be waited on by Riva. This attention was enough for friendship. He lived as a baby in the cradle of her attention. She gave him everything he wanted.

LITTLE JACK

It is easier to build strong children than to repair broken men.
—Frederick Douglass

Everyone wonders why there is a Big Jack and a Little Jack in our family. Everyone can note the gentle, loving personality of Little Jack and remember the gentleness of Riva, our mother. And everyone remembers the stories of the beatings Yalek received from Babe Fradle.

I remember hearing from my mother, Riva, who told us many stories of our family in Baranovka, about Baba and Jacob and their children. What an unusually devoted family this was—how they loved their father, Jacob, and respected him, how they respected and were devoted to one another.

Riva and her siblings loved and respected their father, Jacob, a learned man and scholar. They tried to live and emulate his philosophy of humaneness for themselves and their children. They were exceptionally generous people. Because all the children had decided to name all their firstborn male sons after Jacob, there were four Jacks in our family. The first two were Big Jack and Little Jack. Next came Herman's son, who was named Jack, but everyone called him Sonny. And then Ben had a son named Jack Sherman.

My brother, Little Jack, was born in the two-story house my father bought. He was a beautiful child, with Riva's looks and personality. He was a happy child, like Yalek, with a great sense of humor and wit. As he grew up in his teens, he became interested in theater and had good acting ability.

Jack learned Yiddish as his first language, as I did. He learned English when he started school. He then had difficulty reading. But this was never diagnosed so my parents did not know about it, and in those days, there were no adequate services for remediation as there are today. The result was that he went through school with good intelligence and ability, but with poor development of language and reading.

When Jack and I attended the Yiddish shul, Jack was a good student. He learned Yiddish easily and learned to read all the literature in Yiddish. He was a good reader in Yiddish.

After graduating from the local high school, Jack went to work for the US Army Signal Corps, at Fort Monmouth as a technician. He had learned many skills from our father Yalek, a talented builder. He adapted these skills to work at the army base.

By then it was 1940. The United States was preparing for World War II. Jack was working at the Signal Corps, where he had met and fallen in love with Sophie. Sophie was working as secretary to the military officers at Fort Monmouth. She was a pretty woman who lived with her mother and family in Long Branch, the town adjoining Fort Monmouth.

Jack was drafted into the US Army. He served two years in the European front. When he returned, he and Sophie decided to marry. They lived in an apartment in Belmar, given to them by our father, Yalek.

Sophie's mother, Philomena was divorced from her father. She owned a grocery store in the neighborhood populated by blacks and Jews. She had five children. She was a woman of strong opinion with regards to race and taught her children to hate black people (and the Jews, too). This bigotry permeated most of her conversations with her children. She was opinionated as well.

After a few years, Sophie and Jack had two daughters, Nina and Lisa. Our father, Yalek, helped them to buy a large house in a town near Fort Monmouth. Jack still lives in the house.

We visited them as often as we could. We lived near Boston, which was six hours away. Over the years, we listened to the complaints about their children. Both girls had finished high school and college. Both had attended a college with a religious affiliation. Both met and married young men who were attending the same college. Lisa was unhappily married.

There were many issues that they needed professional help with. However, Sophie, like her mother, did not believe in professional help.

Almost daily, at the dinner table, the conversation turned to Jack's difficulties with the English language. Jack was not knowledgeable. He spoke slowly; he made many linguistic errors. He was slow in reading and often poor in pronouncing words. And he had difficulty writing. These problems should have been corrected when he was young. But unfortunately they were not identified by the teachers in the early grades. And remedial help was not offered when he was in school.

Jack was a gentle, soft, loving person. He was the image of Riva, our mother, the most loving person. I spoke to Jack about the humiliation he was suffering in being criticized so cruelly by Sophie and his daughters. He was embarrassed but said he could not say anything to help them understand his situation. His way was to leave the room, go to the next room, and cry. He was unable to tell them. I was concerned for him.

Nina, the older daughter, had two children, a son and a daughter. When they grew up, Jack paid for their college educations and all the expenses.

Now, many years later, Sophie has died. Jack lives alone. Neither his daughters, nor his grandchildren, call to speak to him. He is ninety-two.

I can only remember the stories that Riva told about Babe Fradle, Yalek's mother, and how she beat him when he was growing up and sent him to sleep in the chicken coop. I believe the result of this was that he became inarticulate and could not talk to Riva, his wife, or to us, his children, whom he loved passionately.

I remember my obsessive memories about Yalek. Sad and sobering, his was a journey from the hub of darkness, when every morning, he wrapped his pillow in its blanket and put them both in the bedroom, when the enthusiasm of life had reached its delusional moments. I see Jack now; he resembles the beauty of Riva and Yalek, but the blush of his spirit has gone—a most happy person who always made jokes and sang every song from every musical show on Broadway. What happened to this most happy fellow?

I remember growing up with Jack. His love of people and enthusiasm for life, both of which he inherited, have given way to despair. Yalek never told us how he loved Riva. We could feel it, see it in his eyes. He did not learn to say, "I love you." But Little Jack knew how to say it. And we knew that Riva loved Yalek.

BIG JACK: A LIFE FULFILLED

No one who is not diseased could be so insanely cruel.
—William Carlos Williams

Willa Cather once observed that in all families, the struggle to have anything of one's own, to be one's self at all, creates a strain. Even in harmonious families, there is this double life—the group life, which we can observe, and whatever private life we can grasp. Human relationships are a tragic necessity of human life; half the time, every ego is greedily seeking them and the other half, defensively pulling away.

The last time I spoke to Big Jack was in March 2011, just before he died. He was in the hospital in Palisades Park, California. It was just after he had a stroke. He called me from the hospital, and I called him several times after. Usually he called me every weekend and called my brother at the same time.

I had spoken to my brother and knew that Big Jack was near the end. There was a slight tremor in his voice. His voice was still strong, just like when he was young, like the general in charge. It reminded me of when he was young, and "the brightest" in the family—or so everyone thought.

His weekly call started with "how's your health?" Then he asked, "How is your weather?"

Of course, he really did not need to know the answers. He already knew the weather. Jack always checked the weather map for the world every morning. He then would tell us what the weather was. This was the engineer, "the general" speaking.

We were raised as children of one family—our mothers were sisters; our fathers were brothers. The families grew up together in Baranovka. Riva and Yalek had married there. After they arrived in the United States, they all lived together in the house that Yalek rented. I was born there. My cousin Big Jack was born there. Ida was not married. She found herself pregnant. Everyone in the family knew that Harry was the father.

As I mentioned earlier, Jack was a beautiful child; he had a round face and deep-set, dark eyes. He looked just like Harry; he was tall and well built. He was extremely bright, and after he graduated from high school with all A's, he attended MIT, where he received an MA in Electrical Engineering.

Immediately after, he went to Princeton to work for the Institute of Science, a new group assigned to develop the A-bomb by the government. Jack was the mathematician on the computer. It was at the institute that he met Albert Einstein, who asked Jack to build a super-record player, one with utmost sound reproduction. Jack and Frances met every weekend with Einstein and his wife. They listened to classical music on Jack's recorder while they discussed politics.

After five years, Einstein advised Jack to leave the institute. Jack left and went to California to work for Hewlett-Packard, car manufacturer. He lived in Palisades Park, a suburb of LA, with Frances, his wife, and their two children, Barbara and Carl. Big Jack called my brother, Jack, to chat every weekend. He called me to chat. The conversation was always the same, "How is your health?" "What is your weather?" It was always the same for me and my brother—a standard conversation. We know that he loved my Jack. They were close, like brothers, growing up. Big Jack considered himself the more intelligent one, but he loved Little Jack as his little brother. And he always considered that he must take care of his little brother.

In retrospect it seems he needed both of us. He needed the closeness he had with us as we were growing up together. Living together with us, with the two brothers and two sisters as parents, he built his security of family on the four of us together. And he had a special attachment to my mother, Riva, who raised him as a little child and who was so good to him after Ida died.

My brother, Jack, and Big Jack and his sister, Freda, and I all grew up together. During summer, we all lived together in Yalek's house in

Belmar, where Riva took care of us. We all slept on the open porch under the dark sky filled with stars, listening to the rolling, banging waves and feeling the salty spray on our cheeks. That was the most dreamy sleep a child could imagine. We ate daily Baba's baked fish and vegetables daily from the local fishermen's catch. And we swam in that wonderful, calming ocean twice a day.

Big Jack grew up with his parents, Ida and Harry, in New Brunswick where Harry inherited the grocery store after Sam's sudden death. Harry had no previous training as a businessman. The grocery store was in a Hungarian neighborhood and catered to a Hungarian working-class population; it sold all kinds of grains, coffee, tea, and sugar by the pound. The biggest group of customers was the bootleggers. They bought the natural grains to make whiskey.

Although he was previously not a business man, Harry's personality was suitable. He was an easygoing, large, affable man who just liked to have a good time. He was "a natural" in the business of supplying the bootleggers. Their friendship was solid. The money came rolling in—all cash.

Harry came home at noon every day for his dinner and a nap on the sofa. Because of his large size and the narrowness of the sofa, his frame would hang over the edge. His pocket opened; the cash spilled out. The bills would spill out all around. The children had great fun picking up the bills, like a Marx Brothers comedy.

Ida was a petite woman, like her mother, Baba. She was exceptionally talented; she had inherited the talent for design and for visual arts from Jacob. She was a talented dress designer. This had been evident from her early years. She designed and made clothes for the entire family when she was a young girl. When she arrived in New York City at eighteen, she soon found a job as a sample maker. She was cultured, like all of Jacob's children, and knew about music, art, and all the cultural events available in the city. And because there was considerable money when she was working, she always bought the tickets for us to attend the concerts. We went to the Philharmonic Symphony concerts for children at Carnegie Hall regularly. We attended the concerts of the New York City Ballet regularly. And we went to all the art museums regularly.

All of Baba Bella and Jacob's children were intellectuals; all were classical music buffs; all knew about art. When Big Jack was a little boy, he was already listening to the New York Philharmonic Orchestra every day. He had his own record player and records. And when he was in high school, he was building his own sound system. This system cost about $2,000. But there was plenty of money from the success of the grocery store.

Jack had few friends in high school—perhaps one whom I remember. But he did not want friends. He was always a loner, satisfied to be alone in his room, listening to his music that he played loud. Until the neighbors called the police.

He did not socialize with other children or adults. His parents were not concerned. Being immigrants, they did not notice. As family, no one dared to criticize "his highness."

Stepping back a generation to Harry as Babe Fradle's son, Harry grew up in Baranovka, as Babe Fradle's second son after Yalek. He was a large man—good-looking and overweight. He loved eating, and he loved sex. He was Babe Fradle's favorite son. She never punished him like she punished the other children, especially Yalek, whom she beat. She favored Harry, and she spoiled him. When the family arrived in United States, they all lived together in the house on Lamberton Street in Trenton. Harry was single. Ida was a beautiful young woman; she was Riva's sister with a good job in New York City as a sample maker in the garment industry. One does not need to try very hard to imagine what happened next.

Big Jack was born to Ida. Harry was the father. She was distraught. Harry became a father. He was ecstatic. Jack was a most beautiful child. And he was "bright." Harry idolized his child. He was a parent, and he was generous. He had lots of money from the bootleggers. Soon Harry and Ida and Jack lived in a nice home, a one-family house, with big yard. Ida, with her designer's ability, soon made outstanding furnishings of imported Belgian linen fabric—linen drapes and bedspreads and chair covers. And then there was the garden—the most exquisite ever seen.

In their house, there were four bedrooms. One for Ida and Harry, one for Jack, and one for Freda and me to share. Our room was adjacent to Ida's. Jack's room was at the front of the house, adjacent to the sunroom, facing the street and neighborhood. It was far removed from the middle of the house. Jack would close the door and play his records at full blast until the neighbors called the police. In our room, we could hear the arguing and the screaming.

I knew that my mother knew what was happening. The family knew. Jack was always a straight-A student. There was no question that he was a near genius. From an early age, he was obsessed with electrical engineering. He applied early to MIT and was accepted. Then he stayed on for a masters degree. When he finished MIT, the family learned that Ida was ill with breast cancer. She was operated on. We learned that the cancer had spread to the brain. She remained at home, cared for by my mother and Rachel, Yalek's sister, and a nurse. With Riva and Rachel as caregivers, Ida lived eleven months. She was forty-one when she died. She left two children, Jack and Freda.

For this devoted family of immigrants—Baba, Riva, and the four siblings remaining—this was the most aggrieved tragedy that could be imagined. Sam, the youngest, had been killed at age twenty-six by a drunk driver. And then Ida—so brilliant, so talented, so beautiful, so much to live for—was dead at forty-one. This was total anguish.

One cannot describe the grief, the sorrow, of this young, completely devoted, immigrant family. The loss that everyone lived through changed existence into a life without hope. There was no recall of the dead. For this young, devoted family, the crisis of Ida's sudden death was beyond comprehension.

Some months after Big Jack's death, I had the pleasure of talking to his son, Carl, who told me what a wonderful mother Frances was. From early on, she taught them to love nature, to know about birds, animals, the earth, and the seas. Frances took them camping at an early age. She taught them to love books and reading. She was a librarian. And Carl told the story of Jack's obsession with psychiatric problems.

Almost every week, he insisted that Frances must go for psychiatric help.

Not just to see the psychiatrist, but to be admitted to the psychiatric ward for treatment; After many years, this had its effect. Frances's system broke down and she died. Carl was also sent for psychiatric help by his father. The last time Carl saw the psychiatrist, the doctor said to him, "It is not you who needs help. It is your father who needs psychiatric help."

Big Jack had difficulty establishing close relationships. He never had close friends. Socially, he did not relate to other human beings. He lived in his own closed world, listening to classical music all his life. There was no normal relationship with his children. Carl attests to this. Jack was authoritarian, imperialistic, and cruel. He knew only how to be an authoritarian father, to give orders. He did not show love and did not know how to love.

Jack was narcissistic from the time he was a young child. His father, Harry, only knew how to give him lots of money, but he never talked to him, played with him, spent time with him, or got to know him. He raised Jack, his son, to be self-interested, selfish. He raised him like his mother Babe Fradle raised Harry, by spoiling him. She did not show her children how to love. They did not know how. This is what the Babe Fradle personality brought into the second generation.

My brother and I remember Big Jack as a beautiful little boy, exceptionally bright, maybe brilliant. We remember him as an intelligent man, accomplished in his field of engineering. But he was self-interested and self-involved. He was never interested in anyone else.

His own family relationship with his children suffered. In the end, he died alone with his housekeeper. Both his children, Barbara and Carl, were eliminated from his will. He left his house and money to his housekeeper.

When Carl talks about his father, he only shakes his head. We all feel the pull from Babe Fradle.

THE YEARS WITH EINSTEIN

It was 1941. Big Jack was finishing his master's degree in electrical engineering at MIT. There was much talk of war in the country. Many people seemed edgy, some were fearful. Jack's mother, Ida, died the year before, in July 1940. After she was diagnosed, we knew the cancer had metastasized. She was attended around-the-clock by Riva and Rachel and a nurse. They kept her alive for eleven months with their excellent nursing care. We were barely able to accept the terrible tragedy of her death. Many of us are still grieving.

We were totally paralyzed by this immeasurable grief. Our family was not prepared for such tragedy to happen to such a young, healthy person. It was the heart of darkness, the very depth. Ida was the shining star of our small, devoted family. Everyone, not just her family, knew her as an exceptional human being. She was exceptionally generous and kind.

For Big Jack, the loss of his mother at such a crucial time in his life was a great tragedy. He was still very attached to her. He had not yet separated from her. He was still totally focused on himself, like a young child, and dependent on her for complete support. Luckily, my mother, Riva, who was considered the head of the family, was there to provide support for him.

Freda, who still needed to finish her college education, was also in need of support. She was sixteen when her mother died. Riva and I became her support system; we were her surrogate mothers. We all lived together, and we provided parenting for Ida's children.

It was at this critical time that Jack met Frances. She was from a family in northern New Jersey. They were married soon after Jack got the job at the Institute for Advanced Study in Princeton. Jack was the chief mathematician working on the computer for the A-bomb with Jon von Neumann. The technical computer and engineering work for the war preparation took place at Princeton.

Jack loved the work; it was pure science for him, and he excelled. He knew he was good. He was more interested in numbers than people. Jack loved living in Princeton. It was an intellectual community. He felt he fit in. Frances also enjoyed the community of academic people.

Shortly after they arrived in Princeton, some of his coworkers discovered that Jack loved classical music and that he loved listening to records of classical music. They also learned that he had built a large recording machine for himself. It was the size of half the dining room.

Someone at the Institute knew that Einstein also loved classical music. And it was Einstein's seventieth birthday. One of his friends told Einstein about Big Jack and his recording machine. Einstein sent a message to Jack to meet. They met, liked each other, and became friends. Then Einstein asked Jack to build the same machine for him. His friends gave him this recording machine for his birthday gift. Einstein and Jack used to meet every Saturday, with their wives, to listen to the records. Einstein loved listening to records and discussing politics.

Jack loved to play his records excessively loud. When he lived at home, in the corner bedroom, he played the music so loud that the neighbors complained. But his parents did not stop this.

Jack told me that Einstein suggested it was time for Jack to leave the Institute.

Einstein was against the war. He was also against the use of the A-bomb. He reasoned that Japan knew they were defeated and were going to surrender.

Soon afterward, Jack left the Institute. He had obtained a job with Hewlett-Packard in California. Jack and Frances moved to California.

Soon after they moved to California, Frances and Jack had two children, Barbara and Carl. Both children were mathematically gifted and brilliant students, inheriting their father's intellectual, mathematical, and scientific ability. In addition, both children were interested in nature, like their mother, Frances. They considered themselves naturalists. As soon as they finished college, both Barbara and Carl went to the woods and went to work for the US Forest Service.

Frances was a librarian; she worked in the high school. She loved camping; she was an expert and knew all about it. She and Jack took the children on camping trips frequently.

Both Barbara and Carl had bad experiences as children growing up with their father, Jack. He was overly rigid, opinionated, domineering, and overpowering, and he never allowed them to have their own opinions. He also had a bad temper. I remember the stories of Babe Fradle, that she was rigid, domineering, and tyrannical.

Both children reported that their parents had a difficult relationship almost their entire married life. There was severe strain between them because of Jack's domineering narcissistic personality and bad temper. He blamed everyone else.

He insisted that Frances should be hospitalized for psychiatric care. Finally, Frances became weakened by the accusations that she was mentally ill (never confirmed). She had been subject to a lifetime of psychiatric hospitalization. She finally died. After her death, both Barbara and Carl became further estranged from Jack. He continued to insist that both children had psychological problems and needed psych care.

Jack died on March 2012. He left a will excluding his two children, Carl and Barbara. He left his estate of several million dollars to his housekeeper, a woman who had prepared his meals.

FREDA

The butterfly effect: A random casually ruled individual lives. And how one unlucky event can set off an unexpected chain reaction. Whereby the flapping of a tiny butterflies wings can supposedly lead to a huge storm.

—Penelope Lively

The past molds—or fails to mold—the present and the outcome of one's own life seem so arbitrary.

Freda was the baby of the four of us. As children, we were one family. Freda was sixteen when her mother, Ida, died. She still had to finish college, so Riva and I served as surrogate mothers after that.

I remember an incident one afternoon when Freda was eight. We were living in the apartment on Handy Street. She was playing with Miriam, her close friend and neighbor. She came up to our bedroom; she was angry about something. She opened the closet door, where her eight dresses were hanging, stiffly ironed, like statues. She threw them on the floor, stepped on them until they were wrinkled and dirty, and stomped out.

Ida was upset, totally despairing. She wanted Freda to understand that Mrs. Mac, the housekeeper, had worked hard to wash and iron her clothes, and she must be appreciative that they could afford to have Mrs. M. There was no word of disapproval from her father, Harry.

In raising Freda, her father had spoiled her completely from the time she was born. She was a beautiful child, with big blue eyes, like Harry's. He knew no other way, and he was making lots of money from the bootleggers. He showered both Jack and Freda with money. They were driven to school. They were driven to concerts and anywhere they needed to go. It was the money that molded their lives. "A tiny butterfly's wings."

In Jack's case, the spoiling was related to his lack of understanding of another person. For Freda, it was somewhat better. She was very kind and generous; she had many friends and loving relationships with her family, with us.

Freda finished college with a major in music. She worked for two years at the Columbia University Library. She met Eliot, who was also living in New Brunswick. After a short courtship, they were married.

Eliot grew up in New Brunswick. His father had been an electrician; his mother owned a stationary store. He was going to NYU to become a security analyst. Eliot was determined to become rich. He was very smart. He understood the financial system and Wall Street. Eliot was a highly determined man.

He watched his mother work hard in her paper store, and he watched her grow old and sick. He decided that Freda should stay at home to raise the children. Freda stayed at home. They raised their children: Rebecca, a lawyer; Adam, a lawyer and the Mayor of Long Branch; and Daniel, a security analyst. All three were successful. Eliot died of cancer at age seventy-eight. Freda died two years later of a staphylococcus infection she picked up after a spinal operation. She was seventy-six.

I lived with Freda, as a sister and caregiver, since the day she was born. Freda lived with everyone as her mother Ida taught her—with generosity and caring and love. She was talented, like Ida, and an expert in gardening, growing the most beautiful flowers, and decorating, as Ida did, with exquisite colors, fabric, and furnishings.

As a young girl, she was very beautiful, resembling Babe Fradle with her sparkling blue eyes. Everyone understood that she was spoiled by Harry and had inherited his temper. Among the four of us, she was caring, kind, and giving. She cared for us when needed. She was devoted, like Ida with her siblings, and like Babe Bella and Jacob, her grandparents.

Unlike Jack, who developed narcissism, which affected his life and relationships, the butterfly effect was an unlucky effect that could set off unexpected chain reactions. In Freda's case, "it only ripple[d] through the flow of life."

Freda and Eliot's children, Rebecca, Adam, and Daniel, are kind and caring individuals. They are generous and loving. They will carry on the legacy of the female sea, as Melville observed.

They may have escaped the random effect of Harry's spoiling and of Babe Fradle's short temper.

CHAPTER VII

MCCARTHYISM; OUR HEART OF DARKNESS

"I'd Hate Myself in The Morning" Is the title of a memoir by Ring Lardner Jr, who was the last surviving member of the Hollywood Ten, that well known intrepid band of screen writers, who were subpoenaed before the House Committee on Un-American Activities Committee (HUAC) by Senator Joseph McCarthy. It was the 1950's, the time of "anti-communist hysteria, Harry Truman's Loyalty programs and Joseph McCarthy 's treason charges, known as the McCarthy "Witch Hunts". It was ostensibly to find spies in the government. It was meant to help Truman get re elected. This was an eloquent memoir, a scrupulous cultural history of the time, better known as a surreal time.

Ring Lardner Jr. was one of four sons of Ring Lardner, the legendary sportswriter newspaper columnist (and best friend of F. Scott Fitzgerald) He was known for his "dazzling ability with language" and his great sports writing. The Lardner sons inherited their father's hatred of hypocrisy and magical ability with words. Virginia Wolf "saw him as a literary pioneer. There were four sons, all writers. This was Ring Lardner Jr.'s answer to the Huac Committee, in response to the House Committee Chairman's' question about membership. As a result he was cited with "contempt". But the Committee continued. McCarthyism was continued under the Truman presidency.

The McCarthy era of the 50's was the most widespread episode of political and cultural repression in the history of the United State. "It was a bad time for freedom." (from Ellen Schrecker, historian) "It cast a wide shadow over America's political life." It was a crusade conducted by Joe McCarthy mainly against government employees. Many careers were ruined, many marriages and even lives were ruined.

Bern was a government employee, at the US Army Base, at Ft. Monmouth, where the McCarthy Hearings were held. He was one of the group of engineers removed from his job because of the McCarthy hunt. There were thousands of teachers, longshoremen, civil servants put on trial, lost their jobs, and ended up on blacklists. The anti-communist crusade, against the government employees ruined many careers, many marriages and even lives. There were thousands of teachers, longshoremen, union leaders, civil servants, who were put on trial lost their jobs, and ended up on blacklists, For many families that was the end, their lived were destroyed.

I was married to my great love, Bern for more than sixty years. We met and fell in love at end of summer, at the ocean in Belmar, where my father Yalek had built a summer house. We walked on the boardwalk under the stars, with the ocean spray in our faces. Since he has gone every day that passes I love him more.

Our marriage was arranged by his father Isaac, a most extraordinary man. He was handsome, with white hair and wonderful face with sparkling blue eyes. A man of great intellect and culture with immense love of children. a human being unparalleled. With his love of family. Bern inherited Isaac's handsomeness his wonderful face, as well as his intellect, and culture. Bern was above all else a devoted family man. He was passionately in love with his family.

Our meeting was arranged by Isaac after attending my Aunt Ida's funeral. Isaac and Lisa. Bern's parents had been friends with Ida and my parents ever since my family arrived in the US as immigrant. Isaac asked Bern to come meet me. He told Bern "She needs someone to take care of her." As Bern stepped out of the car, I saw this beautiful young man with curly dark hair and sparkling blue eyes. I fell in love. He saw a shapely well tanned young woman with light blonde hair. He fell in love.

That first night we walked on the boardwalk under the stars, listening to the breaking, roaring waves. With the salt spray on our faces. He held my hand tightly in his. For the rest of our lives.

Bern was an engineer, with two degrees in Mechanical Engineering. At the time we met he was working for the U.S. Civil Service Commission in NYC.

When the WAR build up started he was transferred to the US Army Signal Corp, at FT. Monmouth. (N.J.) There he was made Director of Hiring engineers and scientists for the military forces for the war. And not long after, he was drafted into the US Navy.

This was totally unexpected. Bern had loss of hearing in both ears ever since childhood. It was 50%, 40%. It was due to frequent ear infections as a child. There was no antibiotics at that time the doctor treated each infection by piercing the ear drum for drainage. With the result that the eardrum became with scar tissue, and that reduced the ability to vibrate. In spite of the hearing loss in both ears, Bern graduated high school at age 15, and college at 19, with MA at 20. He was exceptionally bright.

With this medical history we thought the army would not want him. But, the Draft Officer found that Bern was a very experienced engineer. And he drafted him for the Navy, which needed engineers.

We were married on a week end of his leave. It was 1942. We were a loving couple with two bright and beautiful children living in The Vail Homes, a government built housing complex for engineers and families. It was filled with over 400 families of engineers raising children., an idealic child-centered community.

Bern was doing the work he loved. He was loved and well respected by everyone, the military staff and the civilian staff. Everyone knew him as an exceptional individual, exceptionally well trained and competent.

Life was beautiful. I spent my days with our young children, reading stories, playing records, singing songs, playing rhyming games and dancing. Our children thrived. Each one became a fierce reader. They became high achieving students. High achieving adults.

We were secure. Life was serious for those who had been raised in the Depression.

In 1945 President Roosevelt died suddenly. He was succeeded by Harry Truman the Vice-President. The Cold War was in full swing. Joe McCarthy, Senator from Wisconsin, well known conservative was head of the special sub-committee for investigating employees accused of spying. In 1947 Truman had instituted legislation requiring "Loyalty Oaths" of all government employees. It was McCarthyism in full force.

In 1954, the U.S. Army-McCarthy Hearings were held at Ft. Monmouth. These were conducted by Senator McCarthy and his two well-known Aids. (Cohen and Shine) The Hearings were Televised daily. It created a climate of fearfulness and terror across the country. And mostly among the military personnel at the Ft. Monmouth.

That day, Bern came home from work with the notice that he was being removed from his job, and his security clearance was being removed. He was being removed and sent to sit in a far corner of the barracks, empty, with no job. This was the final blow! I was afraid Bern was near destruction.

Knowing what an extraordinary man Bern was, Knowing that the military staff knew that he was extraordinary super loyal, committed to his government job, it was difficult for us to understand what happened. How could this disastrous act fall on him?

At home with the children he tried to maintain utmost strength, atmosphere of normalcy, family. But he was suffering enormous pressure, emotionally and psychologically. The humiliation was incomparable, he was being torn apart by the ego deflation and belief in himself. He was being torn by "fear" and "terror", for himself and for his family. This was unimagined fear and terror for our small loving family.

Bern suffered from "paranoia" for the rest of his life. He was constantly in fear that something would happen to him and he would not be able to take care of us. He lived with fear the rest of his life. Bern was above all else a devoted family man, passionately in love with his family. He was proud of his family, and afraid for them.

Before the Army-McCarthy Hearings at Ft Monmouth, Bern was at the beginning of a good career. He was prepared with all the experience and talents and intellect. And he was well liked by the military staff and the civilian staff. But he was almost destroyed by the psychological, emotional and social damage of the witch hunt. He saw this as the end of his career.

But, the real damage was to our strong devoted family. Bern felt this as the ultimate damage. The strain of family ties was devastating, and despairing. It lasted what seemed like forever. What remained was Bern's overwhelming feeling to take care of us.

In our case, as victims of the U.S. Army-McCarthy Hearings held at Ft. Monmouth, 1954. Bern suffered for the rest of his life. Our children suffered, missing the relationship of their most loved father, who did not have time to spend with them. Bern's life was driven by his working two jobs for the next twenty years. He was above all else a devoted family man. He was passionately in love with his family.

I read Conrad, and I remember the helpless fear of those days, when Bern was taken out of his job at Ft. Monmouth., because of the US Army McCarthy Hearings. He was sent to sit in an empty barracks building, with no job. It came as total shock. It was unimagined terror and fear for us, for our small family but mostly for Bern.

The memory rolls on like in Conrad. There was darkness there was fear, it was terrifying. As Conrad said, there was no answer. We were helpless and insecure for the rest of our lives, and the fear continued into the third generation. Into the life of our only granddaughter.

Our lives were driven by the fear in the country, by the McCarthyism that engulfed the nation for the next twenty years, and more. It was as

Conrad said "It was very simple, it blazed at you, terrifying." Hiding under the bed in fear of what McCarthy would do to us. Very few people, living today, can understand the enormity of the damage to the person of Bern. Bern was a pinnacle of strength to us, and everyone who knew him.

We were a loving couple with two bright and beautiful children living in The Vail Homes, a government built housing complex for engineers families. It was filled with families raising children, an idealic child-centered community.

Bern was doing the work he loved. He was well respected, and loved by all the military associates and civilian staff. Everyone knew him as an exceptional individual. An exceptional competent person.

Life was beautiful; I spent the days with our young children, reading stories, playing records, singing songs, playing rhyming. Our children thrived. Each one became a ferocious reader. They were high achieving students, and adults as well. We felt secure. Life was serious for those of us who had been raised in the Depression of the 30's.

In 1945 President Roosevelt died suddenly. He was succeeded by Harry Truman. The Cold War was in full swing. Joe McCarthy was a Senator, who headed the investigations known as McCarthy "witch Hunts". It was 1947 when Truman instituted the legislation requiring a "Loyalty Oath" of all government employees. All employees were suspect.

It created a climate across the country of fearfulness and terror. Not only among the general population but especially among the military at Ft. Monmouth.

Arthur Miller, the most renowned playwright of the time said, "The color and the tone of that era are hard to convey. It was a time of national convulsions." The purpose of creating the fear and terror was to disarm the society.

At Ft. Monmouth, the day McCarthy opened the Hearings, Bern came home with the notice that he was being removed from his job.

And that his "security clearance" taken away. He was removed from his work and sent to the far end of the Ft. Army Base, to sit in an "empty barracks" without work. No reason given. He remained in limbo.

Knowing what an extraordinary man Bern was, and knowing that the military staff knew Bern to be a super loyal, super committed engineer for the government, it was difficult for us to understand how this could happen to him. For Bern it was inconceivable to be accused without cause. Or, to be regarded as disloyal. He was nearly destroyed.

The darkness effect: At home and with the children I watched as Bern tried every day to maintain with utmost strength the atmosphere of normalcy, of family. But he was under enormous pressure, emotionally about his status at work. He was suffering from awful humiliation of the "accusation'", and his ego, and belief in himself, his position of engineer, highly regarded by the military staff and civilian staff, and as father to his children. He was a torn man, He became a driven man. He suffered extreme fear and paranoia, he was insecure and scared. But, he needed to be strong, to assure his children and family that they were safe and that he would take care of us. This is what I observed, daily.

Bern loved his job working for the government. He was proud of his record of many years. But his great fear, was his concern for his family and his ability to work and provide for us. This was the focus of his life. This was his surviving strength. This he inherited from his father Isaac. Isaac taught him love and responsibility.

Bern was strong. Bern was a survivor. A survivor from two strands: one, as a child he was absolutely loved by his parents. He had confidence in himself. And as a young teen, he would go every Saturday to his Dad's office and do the bookkeeping, He took care of all the accounting. He was very bright, gifted in math. And he was undaunted as a young boy growing up with Isaac.

For a long time after the children were born, Bern had been thinking of a business to supplement the income from the government job. With this devastating blow, and his job loss, it seemed to open the door for Bern to pursue his plan for a business.

During the build up of the war, Ft. Monmouth increased its personnel many fold. It was Bern's idea that the town adjoining the base was a good location for a Bowling Alley. He knew the area. He talked to the local real estate people. They agreed with him. For the next three years he traveled extensively to investigate the newly built bowling alleys, with the new machinery just coming into the market.

Bern located the exact location. He did the financial planning (remember his experience with the book-keeping and accounting). And when all the plans were done including the legal plans, Bern found a small group of investors. They accepted, they were happy to invest. They appointed Bern as Manager.

Bern did not leave his government job. He just added another job as Manager of the Bowling Alley. Then life became work, work, around the clock. Every day he went to his government job. Then came home for dinner, took a short rest, then went to work. He came home after closing the business, usually at 2 a.m. Bern worked this schedule, of around the clock, for the next ten years. At home, I worked as teacher, and the children went to school. Our children saw us as "workaholics". Our lives were driven by work. Our work was driven by fear.

Bern was tired. His life was strained. He was psychologically and emotionally on a tight rope. His personality was strained. He was drained of energy, short tempered and unhappy. He was driven by the long hours of work. He had very little time to spend with the children, or me. He was lonely without the close relationship of his loved ones. There was no family life.

Many historians have written of this period, have recorded the destruction of the McCarthy period, and in particular the disastrous consequences for the many families who were accused. Hundreds of families were hunted by the McCarthy "Witch Hunts" and nearly destroyed. Many children's lives were damaged by drugs, by suicide. But the records show that "there were no spies found" It is as if we should have followed Conrad's suggestion, in Heart of Darkness.

"It was very simple, it blazed at you, luminous and terrifying "Exterminate all the brutes!."

Before the Army-McCarthy Hearings at Ft Monmouth, Bern was at the beginning of a good career. He was prepared with all the experience and talents and intellect. And he was well liked by the military staff and the civilian staff. But he was almost destroyed by the psychological, emotional and social damage of the witch hunt. He saw this as the end of his career.

But, the real damage was to our strong devoted family. Bern felt this as the ultimate damage. The strain of family ties was devastating, and despairing. It lasted what seemed like forever. What remained was Bern's overwhelming feeling to take care of me.

In our case, as victims of the U.S. Army-McCarthy Hearings held at Ft. Monmouth, 1954. Bern suffered for the rest of his life. Our children suffered, missing the relationship of their most loved father, who did not have time to spend with them. Bern's life was driven by his working two jobs for the next twenty years. He was above all else a devoted family man. He was passionately in love with his family.

I read Conrad, and I remember the helpless fear of those days, when Bern was taken out of his job at Ft. Monmouth., because of the US Army McCarthy Hearings. He was sent to sit in an empty barracks building, with no job. It came as total shock. It was unimagined terror and fear for us, for our small family but mostly for Bern.

The memory rolls on like in Conrad. There was darkness there was fear, it was terrifying. As Conrad said, there was no answer. We were helpless and insecure for the rest of our lives, and the fear continued into the third generation. Into the life of our only granddaughter.

Our lives were driven by the fear in the country, by the McCarthyism that engulfed the nation for the next twenty years. It was as Conrad says "It was very simple, it blazed at you, terrifying." Hiding under the bed in fear of what McCarthy would do to us. Few can understand the enormity of the damage to the person of Bern.

I was married to my great love, Bern, for more than sixty years. We met and fell in love end of summer at the ocean, walking and holding hands tightly. Since he has gone, every day that passes I love him more. Our marriage was arranged by his father Isaac, a most extraordinary man. He was handsome, with head of white hair, a wonderful strong face with sparkling blue eyes. A man of great intellect, culture, and generosity. A human being unparalleled. Most prominent was his love for his family, his children. Bern inherited Isaac's handsome looks, as well as his intellect.

Our meeting was arranged by Isaac. After my Aunt Ida's funeral. Isaac and Lisa, Bern's parents had been friends with Ida and my parents ever since my family arrived as immigrants. Isaac asked Bern to meet me. He said, "She needs someone to take care of her." As he stepped out of the car, I saw this beautiful young man with curly dark hair and sparkling blue eyes. I fell in love. He saw a shapely well-tanned young woman with blond hair. He fell in love.

That first night we walked on the boardwalk under the stars, listening to the roaring ocean, with the salt spray on our faces. He held my hand tightly in his. For the rest of our lives.

Bern was an engineer with two degrees in Mechanical Engineering.

At the time we met he was working for the U.S. Civil Service Commission in NYC.

When the War started he was transferred to the US Signal Corp, at FT. Monmouth. There he was made Director of hiring engineers and scientists to build up the military forces for the War. And shortly after he was drafted into the US Navy. This was totally unexpected given his severe hearing loss in both ears. We thought the army would not want him. We were wrong. The Navy needed experienced engineers. The Draft Officer told him they needed him.

We were married on a week end of his leave. It was 1942.

We were a loving couple with two bright and beautiful children living in The Vail Homes, a government built housing complex for engineers families. It was filled with families raising children, an idealic child-centered community.

Bern was doing the work he loved. He was well respected, and loved by all the military associates and civilian staff. Everyone knew him as an exceptional individual. An exceptional competent person.

Life was beautiful; I spent the days with our young children, reading stories, playing records, singing songs, playing rhyming. Our children thrived. Each one became a ferocious reader. They were high achieving students, and adults as well. We felt secure. Life was serious for those of us who had been raised in the Depression of the 30's.

In 1945 President Roosevelt died suddenly. He was succeeded by Harry Truman, who had been Vice-President. The Cold War was in full swing. Joe McCarthy was a Senator, who headed the investigations known as McCarthy "witch Hunts". It was 1947 when Truman instituted the legislation requiring a "Loyalty Oath" of all government employees. All employees were suspect.

The U.S. Army-McCarthy Hearings were held at Ft. Monmouth. 1954. McCarthy was calling for investigations of government employees—He claimed were spies.

In the Spring, Senator McCarthy (and his two aides, Cohen and Shine) descended on Ft. Monmouth. The news of the Loyalty Oaths, became televised hearings every day.

It created a climate across the country of fearfulness and terror. Not only among the general population but especially among the military at Ft. Monmouth.

Arthur Miller, the most renowned playwright of the time said, "The color and the tone of that era are hard to convey. It was a time of national convulsions." The purpose of creating the fear and terror was to disarm the society.

At Ft. Monmouth, the day McCarthy opened the Hearings, Bern came home with the notice that he was being removed from his job. And that his "security clearance" taken away. He was removed from his work and sent to the far end of the Ft. Army Base, to sit in an "empty barracks" without work. No reason given. He remained in limbo.

Knowing what an extraordinary man Bern was, and knowing that the military staff knew Bern to be a super loyal, super committed engineer for the government, it was difficult for us to understand how this could happen to him. For Bern it was inconceivable to be accused without cause. Or, to be regarded as disloyal. He was nearly destroyed.

The darkness effect: At home and with the children I watched as Bern tried every day to maintain with utmost strength the atmosphere of normalcy, of family. But he was under enormous pressure, emotionally about his status at work. He was suffering from awful humiliation of the "accusation"', and his ego, and belief in himself, his position of engineer, highly regarded by the military staff and civilian staff, and as father to his children. He was a torn man, He became a driven man. He suffered extreme fear and paranoia, he was insecure and scared. But, he needed to be strong, to assure his children and family that they were safe and that he would take care of us. This is what I observed, daily.

Bern loved his job working for the government. He was proud of his record of many years. But his great fear, was his concern for his family and his ability to work and provide for us. This was the focus of his life. This was his surviving strength. This he inherited from his father Isaac. Isaac taught him love and responsibility.

Bern was strong. Bern was a survivor. A survivor from two strands: one, as a child he was absolutely loved by his parents. He had confidence in himself. And as a young teen, he would go every Saturday to his Dad's office and do the bookkeeping, He took care of all the accounting. He was very bright, gifted in math. And he was undaunted as a young boy growing up with Isaac.

For a long time after the children were born, Bern had been thinking of a business to supplement the income from the government job. With this devastating blow, and his job loss, it seemed to open the door for Bern to pursue his plan for a business.

During the build up of the war, Ft. Monmouth increased its personnel many fold. It was Bern's idea that the town adjoining the base was a good location for a Bowling Alley. He knew the area. He talked to the local real estate people. They agreed with him. For the next three years he traveled extensively to investigate the newly built bowling alleys, with the new machinery just coming into the market.

Bern located the exact location. He did the financial planning (remember his experience with the book-keeping and accounting). And when all the plans were done including the legal plans, Bern found a small group of investors. They accepted, they were happy to invest. They appointed Bern as Manager.

Bern did not leave his government job. He just added another job as Manager of the Bowling Alley. Then life became work, work, around the clock. Every day he went to his government job. Then came home for dinner, took a short rest, then went to work. He came home after closing the business, usually at 2 a.m. Bern worked this schedule, of around the clock, for the next ten years. At home, I worked as teacher, and the children went to school. Our children saw us as "workaholics". Our lives were driven by work. Our work was driven by fear.

Bern was tired. His life was strained. He was psychologically and emotionally on a tight rope. His personality was strained. He was drained of energy, short tempered and unhappy. He was driven by the long hours of work. He had very little time to spend with the children, or me. He was lonely without the close relationship of his loved ones. There was no family life.

Many historians have written of this period, have recorded the destruction of the McCarthy period, and in particular the disastrous consequences for the many families who were accused. Hundreds of families were hunted by the "Witch Hunts" and nearly destroyed. Many children's lives were damaged by drugs, by suicide. But the records show that "there were no spies found" It is as if we should have followed Conrad's suggestion, in Heart of Darkness.

"It was very simple, it blazed at you, luminous and terrifying

"Exterminate all the brutes!."

THE FINAL SORROW

Each on their own, woven into their own webs,
with strands of fear to hold them.
Each on a different tree.
A different species.

The world became gray, thickened with silence.
Only time moved, the solid sea of fear remained.
Voices fell silent, like buttons falling on sand in the night.

The depth of grief cannot be defined, described, or broken.
Watching the river of time, the time for singing
has passed, blurred by tears.

I watched as my beloved was taken from my side,
a murderous falcon at work, by the cruel men
of the hospital, by men of history.

Our disaster defies all speech, defies meaning.
Our children left behind the best part of themselves,
their love. It is the final sorrow.

Poem by Clara Maslow
2013

AFTERWORD

"Everyone knows that the truth can't be told. You have to make it up, else no one will believe you."

"Now small fowls flew screaming over the yet yawning gulf; a sullen white surf beat against its steep sides; then all collapsed, and the great shroud of the sea rolled on as it rolled five thousand years ago." Melville

After many years of being married to Bern, a lifetime of love, and raising two extraordinary children, I returned, at age ninety, to Belmar to sit on a bench on the boardwalk with my brother, Jack. There we watched that magnificent, extraordinary, "masculine" sea, that beautiful ocean with white rolling waves. The mighty ocean we both loved all our lives.

This same ocean—still rolling, crashing, and rolling on the shore— rolled this way five thousand years ago, though we are not the same. Would that I could tell of the "thinkings" from the bottomless blue of the past. The obsessive memories of my lifetime have been dimmed by the difficulties of my life, by the everyday complexities that occur in our relationships, in our loves.

This book is for my father, Yalek, whom it took me many years to understand as a father, as a man, and as my father, who gave us all his love.

This book is to say that I loved him, and that he loved Riva, our mother, passionately all his life, as he loved us, as he took care of us. He was a devoted, loving father.

As Chekhov says, "Life is a tragedy because it is so farcical." And like many of his characters, you find yourself laughing or crying. It was his genius to elicit this paradox so clearly, so humorously.

It took me a long time to know that I loved my father, and that I finally understood him. He had difficulty talking to us; he was inarticulate because of the beatings he received from his angry mother, Babe Fradle, during his young years growing up with her in Baranovka. He could not express his love and caring. But he respected us; he was proud of us and our achievements. All of this was difficult for him. He loved us, and we loved him.

APPENDIX

The last letter from Bern to Emily Cohen, dated February 12, 2000

Dear Em,

We're glad you've gotten to know something of our past history and experiences since they define who we are. On a more personal tack, there was a period shortly before and after we were married, that, together with friends, we would visit a nightclub called Café Society downtown in Greenwich Village. The attraction there was the performances by some of the greatest jazz artists of the time. (Albert Amons, Pete Johnson, Meade Lux Lewis, Mary Lou Williams.) I remember one time in particular that we visited Café Society when I was home on leave from the navy. As we were being shown to a table, it was as though there was a sudden hush in the conversations as heads swiveled around to admire the luminous blonde beauty escorted by the guy in the sailor suit. And I felt a surge of pride that I was privileged to have a share, as did no one else, of this visual work of art. And as the years went on, I was able to feel even greater pride in her accomplishments and engagement with people.

And despite the rocky periods we sometimes went through, as we approach our fifty-eighth anniversary, we can turn to each other and say, "I love you so much; I'm glad I married you, and there is no one else I've met over the years that I would rather have married."

All our love. And if there is anything we can do, you have but to ask.

Love,

Clara and Bern

A letter to Jane, dated May 30, 2006

Bern and I were two exceptional people, both of us were very handsome, intellectually superior, and talented. We come from families that were exceptional. And we had two children also above the standard, exceptionally beautiful, intelligent, and talented.

For fifty years you have honed your writing skills so that you could write to me. You would write to me to keep me away, to not touch me. Particularly over the past forty years, you have written letters telling me what is wrong with me and with psychological diagnosis.

I have known of your excellent writing ability since you were in high school, and writing for the school newspaper. I was aware of your excellent analytical ability. I remember we used to talk at the dinner table every evening. That Bern encouraged you to become a lawyer.

Every letter to me has been another display of your excellent language skills. But always there is a zinger line; (i.e. the daughter that has been vilified is unsuitable. To be rejected and even punished).

I have also known of your talent in drawing. It comes directly from me, from my father, Yalek. When he was a young boy, he used to make beautiful architectural drawings. And I also inherited from my mother, Riva, the designing skills, like Ida, for dressmaking. These come from their father, Jacob, my grandfather.

I have written you many times of my inherited talents from both sides. The talents exhibited in my decorating and in my gardening. And that you have inherited these talents from me.

I have also been a keen observer of people. And I have trained myself to be a creative teacher as you can see from my record in teaching the deaf children.

You were about seven when you began to compete with me for your daddy's attention and his love. It was when you were about twelve that you actually began to let me know—that you wanted to leave me. It was shortly after our experience with the McCarthyism that nearly destroyed Bern.

It was then you showed your dislike for me.

Most people whose families experienced these circumstances with the intense fear are now gone. There were some who wrote memoirs describing the sheer devastation of their lives. Mine is only one.

However the extreme fear and terror that he suffered and the paranoia that he suffered was unique. It revived the paranoia that he suffered when he was a child due to the extreme hearing loss. He built up incredible strength and courage, which helped us to survive this crisis. There were many who did not survive. We were lucky. We had Bern.

In addition to the main concern of making a living, Bern and I were concerned with what happened to our children. What this would do to them. I remember when Jonathan came home one day with his head shaved. Bern and I thought there was something wrong and decided to send him for counseling. In your case, you flatly refused to help me with table chores after dinner. After Bern requested you to help, your constant excuse was, "I have a paper due."

One thing was clear to me, that you had completely withdrawn from our relationship—mother daughter. I knew that you had eliminated me. I knew that I was rejected. But I did not know why.

You never talked to me.

I was under severe stress at my teaching job at Tinton Falls Schools and at home with Bern and his paranoia. I did not know the long-term effects of this fear of McCarthyism.

Then when we got to know Emily, to listen to her story, her own experience. We realized that the fear had spread. That it had reached the third generation. And then I knew that fear has long tentacles that can reach into the next generation. "Fear and anger become an illuminated index of the madness around us." (Arthur Miller)

It was then I realized how deep the roots of fear had invaded our family, its loving relationship, and nearly destroyed us. But in your case there has been a long-held problem with showing affection.

In both our families, Bern's and mine, there has been affection shown all the time. But, it seems that you have difficulty showing any affection with me. It also explains the fact that you see me coldly. Looking at me, your expression is cold, not loving. You have created a myth about me as a monster.

I don't remember the last time you gave me a hug to show me that you loved me. It was a long, long time ago. Maybe not at all. Maybe I just dream the event.

I wish that I could share this frustration with Bern. But I am afraid that he would be driven to deeper despair. It has been obvious that you do not want a relationship with me. Your hate letter to Dear Dad (of 1996) showed us that you were very mixed up in your emotions. And we do not know if it was the McCarthyism that caused this.

Think how much better it would have been had you shared this turbulence with us, like Baba or Riva. Where does all this bitterness come from? Why do you need to punish all of us? Why do you have such difficulty showing love to us? Or why do you have difficulty being affectionate?

Our world of beautiful, bright, and talented children, like heavenly flowers, the essence of our striving, has been blown up. It is painful to think of the end of love of family. It is frightening.

"We do damaging things to people we love, to things we love." (From Adam Rapp, author-director) "Grief plays a large part in my work, and I return to the gulf between parents and their children because it haunts me for a very long time."

"It doesn't end, never will it end." (Gunter Grass.)

P.S. The most important job you have as mother is to show your children how you take care of your mother. Show them how you care every day and how you show your affection to her.

The most important thing we have to do in life is to care for one another.

Your mother,

Clara, with love.

ABOUT THE AUTHOR

I have lived a long lifetime married to my beloved Bern, a most extraordinary man, a man unparalleled as a human being (Shakespeare). I have had a successful career as a professor of education, specializing in evaluating children with dyslexia. And I have turned to writing a memoir about my husband and my experience with the McCarthy witch hunts in the fifties and a book of poems to eulogize my beloved Bern.

Time passes. What's left are memories. Our memories keep the people present and alive. After a long lifetime, I have absorbed many memories. Memories of my family—like those with my father, Yalek—remain as obsessive memories, fond memories of growing up with him and my mother, Riva, and two families living in close proximity, as one.

These are stories of my obsessive memories of my father, Yalek, and our families, grandparents, and parents from Baranovka, Russia. We carry these stories with us in our daily lives; they determine who we are. These narratives are my observations of the real people, my ancestors, whose stories have influenced my life. I have listened to these stories, across the generations, from the individuals. It is as if someone peeled off the skin of my psyche and exposed the fault lines, as if I wanted to know everything that happened in order to change what went wrong. And there were hurtful wrongs.

But I was looking for meaning as well, for signs of love expressed— the expression of love that my father never taught me. And I never saw. To understand the obsessive memory that I carry of Yalek, the picture of a man carrying his pillow wrapped in a blanket from the living room to the bedroom every morning.

And I wondered why I did not see them, my parents, the most beautiful Riva and the most handsome Yalek together, why I did not hear words of love, and why I did not see affection expressed.

Yalek

Clara sitting on Riva's lap

Lenox lamp designed by Yalek

Jane, Bern, Jonathan, and Yalek

Jane, Jonathan, and Yalek

Bern and Clara Maslow

Bern and Clara Maslow

Bern and Clara Maslow

Clara Maslow